The F

One Child's

Larry Kelly

with James Plaskitt

ISBN 978-1-4709-4445-2

First published in 2011 by The Euston Press
www.thepigeonhouse.info

This is a true memoir, but for privacy, some names have been
changed.

For Shirley

Martin, Andrew and Sharon

"because I would like my family to know"

"lonely I wander through scenes from my childhood"

From the song, 'The Old House'
By Frederick O'Connor

Acknowledgments

It has been a privilege to bring Larry's story out into the open. He is the true author. This is his experience, and what follows is based on his own writings and his oral recollections. I blended together his varied, but always vivid, recollections, and he read, amended, and approved the draft chapters as they emerged. So I readily acknowledge him as the true author, but I also thank him for his diligence and his patience, as I endeavoured to give his words the form that they deserved.

I am also indebted to my good friend Lisanne Radice, who gave much wise advice on the first draft. She set us back to work, and the final result owes so much to her sympathetic guidance.

I am grateful to Carolyn Judd who worked diligently and patiently transcribing the many hours of recorded conversations I had with Larry.

Larry's family were closely involved throughout the process and I am grateful in particular to Shirley for her detailed observations, additional information and all the vital cups of tea along the way. Martin also gave many thoughtful, constructive suggestions. Andrew was there, all the way, providing encouragement and creativity, and making it all possible.

James Plaskitt

Contents

Introduction

Someone paying a brief visit to Dublin early in the 1930s would probably have stood in O'Connell Street, admiring its wide boulevard setting, as fine as any to be found in Europe's capital cities. They may well have proceeded on foot along the wide pavement, passing the rows of elegant shops with their bright awnings, noting the striking column set in the middle of the road, eventually reaching the proud stone bridge straddling the quietly flowing Liffey.

This elegant scene told its own story - of a new state, beset by economic challenges, but still able to present to the world a colourful face of proud defiance.

Had they wanted, or even known, the visitor could, within just minutes, have reached another Dublin. That of the once proud, but now dilapidated, damp and infested Georgian dwellings of the tenements. Once the home of Dublin's prospering merchant classes and even of the lower nobility, these buildings, long since abandoned as their owners emigrated in pursuit of greater wealth, were slowly rotting away as they filled with more and more of Dublin's poor.

Here families of twelve, fifteen, even twenty lived in single rooms, the adults working, if they could, as labourers or dock hands; their ragged, hungry children running about bare-footed in narrow streets in between the cast-off parts of slaughtered animals, the horse manure and the open drains.

Here were uncounted thousands of some of Europe's poorest people, sharing their crowded, cruel space with over 1,000 public houses and over 200 'shebeens' (unlicensed drinking dens), where drink wore away at the edges of the hard realities of regular hunger, eviction, illness and death. In these streets were to be found infant mortality levels over twice that of any of the United Kingdom's largest twenty cities. Diseases such as typhoid and tuberculosis ('consumption') were rife, fuelled by the air trapped over the natural estuary, but suffused with a noxious sulphurous acidity, the product of the locally burnt coal.

Often sitting in pride of place, even in the most overpopulated tenement room, ringing with damp, its ceiling bowed, its walls cracked and its floor bare but for a little sawdust, was the little lamp, glowing red through a glass shade, testament to the ever present obeisance to the Irish Catholic Church. Tenement dwellers would bow to the Priest in the street and the 'Vincent men' – representatives of the St Vincent de Paul charity - would visit the rooms of families to dispense small measures of assistance, provided there was sufficient proof of proper practice and religious observance.   All due solemnity was afforded to the occasion when the small wooden box, draped in a white cloth decorated with little blue bows, was ushered out into the street and onto the back of a horse drawn cart, on route to another infant burial.

Our visitor would not, in all probability, have ventured into this Dublin, where Larry (then known as Lorcan) was born in 1931, the ninth surviving child to John and Mary-Ellen.

His was a childhood disfigured by that other Dublin. His early years of life were spent flitting from one miserable tenement dwelling to another, interspersed by periods in the poor house. Schooling, like decent meals, was intermittent. Later, his attempts, over many youthful years, to escape to a better life were repeatedly frustrated by either his mother or by officialdom.

Between his loveless childhood years and his embattled youth were four years in the Pigeon House. Four years that were for ever after a haunting, black memory. A burden, loaded onto the life of a lonely, innocent child by those into whose care he had been placed, and only lifted, finally, by the telling of the story.

Return to Dublin Bay

The road is narrower than he remembered. Age always seems to shrink childhood spaces. But his memories of the place hold true. And the wind whipping up from the bay was just as keen as he recalled from a time over fifty years before. A blustery, north-easterly which gathers together a sharp salty spray and carries it above and over the low, dome capped south wall.

To one side of him he looks out across the bay toward a home invisible across the horizon. To the other side of him, a tall, weathered brick wall with uneven capping stones loosened by the elements, and hard by them, the roofs of tired buildings darkened by the soot and smuts from the exhausted power station.

His pace is slowed, seemingly, by the wind. A stooped figure approaches him on the other side of the narrow road, hugging close to the wall, itself appearing to lean in sympathy with the wind. An elderly woman, wrapped in a black cloak which flaps against the calves of her grey stockinged legs, and whose protection from the cold air is aided by a white scarf tied tight around her neck. Bent on making progress, and with hands clasped together,

her head stays low. But she catches him a quick, inexpressive glance before once again focusing on the way before her. Pushed forwards by the will to be somewhere.

A strong gust lifts debris from the gutter. It scatters across the road leaving paper, bottle caps and sweet wrappings in new patterns. He wipes the back of his cold bare hands across his face to dry his watering eyes.

As he approaches a point where there is a break in the wall ahead, he pauses. He catches his breath. He feels his pulse quicken. He sees the low, shallow pitched roof close to the wall, with short stubby chimneys just visible above the parapet. Some of the past is present.

Each short renewed step closes down the years. The smell of the air, the sounds of the bay, the buffeting of the wind – they all envelop him. All now, as then. How short the time. But how far his journey.

And now, at last, they are visible. Black gates, in a break in the high wall. Solid black, rusting barriers, held shut with a heavy padlock on a chain. Their strong square frame surrounds diagonal beams with open mesh wire bridging the spaces in between. He stands, as if entranced. He raises one hand and grasps the rusting frame for support. And he peers through.

Piles of bricks, some window frames, gas canisters, pallets. All the belongings of a builder's yard. The plastic sheeting tied loosely over stacks of planks creaks and shifts in the wind. The low, dirty building to his right is a store. An old metal bed frame is propped up against its wall. To the side of the store building, and at a slight angle, is a smaller building with a steeply pitched roof and window frames with distinctly pointed tops. Its narrow, flaking door swings irregularly in the gusts.

As he looks through the wire mesh, the shapes and the colours of the yard before him begin to fade, as if in a mist spilling over from the bay behind. In the haze he sees a small figure in the yard, moving about. A small, thin, wiry figure. A boy, with an outstretched hand.

The wind suddenly bites into the back of his neck and grey dust makes his eyes blink. He does not think the boy can see him. But his own vision is clear. Nothing whatever dims his remorseful, haunting view of the Pigeon House. Or of the road that brought him there.

Chapter 1: No Fixed Abode

I remember her singing – if you could call it singing. There were slurred words, belted out to a sort of tune, its progress punctuated by shouts and belches. It was best to be on your guard. Things tended to fly about a bit. Fridays were the worst. That's when mother would meet my father at tea time as he came out of work and get him to hand over his week's wages. Then she was off to the shebeen with her cronies for the night.

She said she would get us all food. We waited in our room, watching the light fade, waiting for her to appear with a bag full of potatoes and maybe something to boil up for a kind of stew. But in the end, we had to go looking for her. Father would go one way and I went with my brothers in another direction, running in and out of all the drinking dens we knew in the area, looking for her. If we found her at all, it was a real job to get her home. She was so drunk. Often we didn't find her. We would not see her until gone midnight. Then back she would come, rolling about, loud, staggering, and, well, singing.

****

I was told that once, when I was small, we had lived in a house, where there was just about room for us all. But we had to rip the doors off their hinges, break up the furniture and pull up the floorboards, and burn everything in the hearth to keep us warm. She had drunk all the money. We had nothing to buy firewood with. So we were evicted. After that, we went from one tenement room to another. And when she got us thrown out of them for not paying rent, we were in the poor house.

****

I sat on the kerb stone, trailing my toes through the water running along towards the drain further down the road. I clutched the little tin cup close, sometimes waving it about at anyone who came near enough. I would get some scraps. Sometimes they were alright to eat. Coins were rare, but sometimes I would get some. Then I was sure of something to eat before going back to our room. I wouldn't take the money back. There was nowhere to hide it that she wouldn't find.

I hung about at the corner, waiting until the crowds began to thin out a bit. That meant the traders would soon begin to pack up their stalls. The best time to go forward was when I saw them begin to pull out the buckets from under the stall. Then there was a chance. I kept one eye on the trader and his movements, and the other on the other little corners and spaces between the buildings opposite. Mine wasn't the only plan, and I would have to be quick if it was going to work. When there was nobody buying from the stall, I ran out, holding out my metal mug, and banged it on the side of the stall. He was scraping bits off the slab with the back of a large knife, sloshing it into a large bucket. He stopped, sifted through the remains in front of him and picked up a few pieces, tossing them in my direction. I scooped them into my mug. Fish heads could be boiled up into a soup, and if we collected enough between us, we could all eat.

I crawled past and under the other stalls. There were often scraps on the floor, bits of fruit or vegetable that had dropped off the table and got kicked about. It could all go in the pot. Rabbit heads were the best find. But, again, I had to be quick to be sure of getting it.

There were steep stairs going up to our room, and they were dark. The dripping sound was a good guide though. I kept climbing towards it, careful not to lose any of the contents of my tin cup, or drop the leaves clutched between my fingers. The bucket was out on the landing, just next to our room. It caught the constant, slow drip, coming from the roof above.

Middle of the week was best. Mother was in no state to prepare any food we scavenged at the week-end. But by the middle of the week, she had drunk all the money. Whatever we had gathered together was in the pot for our coddle, the best meal of the week. Sometimes the only one.

The room was square and the wooden floor had patches of sawdust in places. The one single window looked out across a yard. There was a stove in one corner, with a few pots bundled against it. Near the window was our table, and two wooden chairs. And then there was our bed, up against the wall, opposite the window, with old coats strewn across it. There was a small lamp on the shelf near the stove. It was lit, when there was any oil to be had, and would give off a red glow, through its coloured shade. Then the faded picture of the Virgin, propped up behind, would seem to stare out through the gloom.

I watched as she poked around at the contents of the pot with a long wooden spoon, tipping in some water collected from the bucket on the landing. She packed some of the peat into the little fire at the bottom, cursing its dampness and casting critical looks at my older brothers, who had brought it home earlier in the day. The fire smoked, rather than burnt and the results of our day's scavenging languished in the tepid water, awaiting the build up of heat below.

Father sat at the table and had first helpings, followed in turn by my elder brothers. I waited. She tipped the pot to its side and scraped about in the bottom with the wooden spoon. She ladled out the steaming broth and its varied contents into a bowl, and passed it over to me, as I stood by the table. My brother handed over the spoon and I began to scoop up the result of our day's efforts.

****

The bucket was not too bad on the way down the stairs. It was the climb back that I dreaded. But out in the yard, I waded across the soaking floor, stepping between the little coloured streams that came out from the corner of the yard where the only toilet was to be found. It was behind a rough wooden door which marked off a corner of the yard. Only the absence of any roof prevented the smells from being too overpowering. Through the door was the bowl, set down on the bare earth, linked to pipes fixed to the side of the house, trailing their way up to a cistern, clinging precariously to the brickwork, and sporting a long rusty chain which, on good days, sent a gush of water down into the pan when yanked hard enough.

I positioned the bucket under the stand pipe and turned the little brass tap. The water began to spill down into the bucket, the sound changing from a rattle at first, to a softer rushing as the level rose. I would watch as the level rose to the point I knew was my limit for heaving it all back up the stairs, then I screwed down the tap and began the trek back. I tried not to lose my footing on the slimy floor of the yard. Provided I got it back without spilling too much on the way, most of us would be able to do a little washing before climbing onto the bed and pulling over the old coats.

****

Word would quickly spread that they were in the area, and likely to drop in. Usually, it was done by other small children running about, saying they were coming. If she was at home, mother would quickly tidy things up and light the little red lamp. She would straighten the picture behind. She sat those of us who were at home on the edge of the bed, after piling the overcoats up on top of one another in the corner of the room. Then she quickly brushed her hair. She put a small chain around her neck and took down the little string of beads that were normally kept on the shelf besides the lamp.

We would hear them coming up the stairs. Then the gentle tap on the door, before it swung open. Mother made us recite, along with her, as she ran her fingers over the beads.

"Hail Mary, full of grace, the Lord is with thee."

The men looked at us, nodding their heads gently as we stumbled through the words. Mother looked them straight in the eye as we reached the end, and began stroking the back of her thumb with her fingers. She would be talking about the last full meal we had, and the problem of getting us to school, and how the damp was so bad this time of the year. We knew that, recitation completed, we had better not say anything more. One of them dipped his hand into his jacket pocket, causing the coins to clink. He handed over a couple of shillings to mother, turned towards us, blessing us, as the other man scratched something into a small notebook with his pencil. They turned and left. Mother put the lamp out.

****

I got the wooden orange crate from one of the street traders, who left it at the side of the road at the end of the day. I was the first to see it. I got it back to our building and hid it behind some broken fencing alongside the yard at the back. There was just enough space to wedge it in, and then cover it with some of the broken wood. I stored it there until I could get hold of some wheels. Eventually, I found them with some scrap that had been piled outside a builder's yard. One was a bit buckled but they turned alright on their simple little axle. Bent nails fastened it to the bottom of the orange box.

The bigger houses were a little way off from our room, but the cart wheeled along alright over the cobbles and broken brick surfaces. I began knocking on the doors, and going round to the back of the grand houses, seeking out the kitchens. Bit by bit, the scraps mounted in the orange crate. I took the better scraps out and they sustained me while I worked my way round the route taking me to enough of the big houses to provide a full load. Once filled, I threw a cover over the contents and began the journey across to Camden Place.

His pigs were in a yard at the back of his house. I looked through the fence that penned them in and watched them snuffling about on the ground with their snouts. He gave me a penny for each bucket load.

****

We were hurried out of the room, each of us given something to carry as we scampered down the stairs. She had drunk the rent money and we were being evicted again. We trouped along, dragging bits of rag on the floor as we went, but holding tight to whatever we had managed to escape with. When we arrived at James Street, the building looked like a castle, set back behind huge wooden gates. We went through the first set, and they were banged shut behind us. We waited in a yard for the second set to be opened. A man came forward and

14

separated us out.   My younger brothers and I headed off to the boys area, my older brothers went with father, and mother went in another direction.

The room had a tall ceiling and the camp beds were crammed in close up against each other.   Meals were served at long tables, where we sat alongside on rough wooden benches.   Mostly, we had soup and sometimes a mug of warm tea.   We played games out in the yard, which was set between our quarters and where the men stayed.   We ran about and sometimes had a ball to kick around.   If we were there in winter time, and the ground was icy, our toes would freeze.   Kicking the ball about with bare feet was painful, particularly if the cold caused a toe nail to split, and bleed.

The boy was pointing up at the roof of the men's building.   We all turned and looked up.   There was a man standing right on the edge, staggering about and he seemed to be shouting something but we couldn't make it out.   He paced up and down, going along the edge of the building, high up above us. He reached out and grabbed the edge of a chimney stack.   He waved his other arm about and kept shouting, tossing his head from side to side.   Then he let go of the chimney and worked his way back along the edge, with one foot in the gutter and the other up a little on the wet tiles.   The game stopped and we stood in a huddle watching the strange man

15

up on the roof above. He yelled again, and waving both arms about, launched himself off the roof. His body whirled through the air, turning again and again. His coat flapped about as he fell. He hit the ground in front of us with a crunching thud, ending up on his front with is face twisted towards us.

The gate to the yard opened and two men came through with long wooden planks. They set them down alongside the body on the floor and rolled it over, positioning it along the wood. Then, each getting hold of an end, they hoisted it up and made for the gateway. They passed in front of us, the planks sagging under their load and drips of blood splashing down onto the ground by our feet.

****

If it was any good, it went to the pawn shop. Mother would take anything, once she had drunk her way through father's wages. Shirts produced enough money for an evening's ale, sometimes more. Even a pan would get a penny or two. Towards the end of the week, trips to the pawn shop became more frequent. It wasn't worth taking home anything good we found in the streets. Better to hide it somewhere. And the same was true of the pennies I earned from my scraps for the pigs. Best hidden if I could, or, if not, spent before getting home. She would be bound to find them if they were anywhere in the room. It was all ale money.

****

Aunt Kitty's kindly face was a bit like a prune, very wizened. She had two rooms in Albert Place, shared with granddad. She and my mother did not hit it off. Mother would sometimes turn up there when I was about, and suddenly launch off at Aunt Kitty, making a terrible scene, as bad as the rows and fights she would start back at our room. I would hide in a corner until it was over or she had stormed off. When she was gone, Aunt Kitty would sigh, smooth down her piny, and pick up her bits and pieces and carry on, smiling down at me.

The seminary was close to where she lived. We would set off together at around tea time, with Aunt Kitty carrying a bag slung over her arm. There was often quite a crowd outside when we got there. We stood and waited. Aunt Kitty would talk with the other women while I sat on the kerb stone. The big black seminary doors would open and a priest emerge. All the bags were passed over to him. With them all bundled under his arm, he went back in behind the black doors. The chattering started again. Then the doors were opened once again, and the bags handed back one by one as they were identified. We walked back home and Aunt Kitty made a meal out of the ends of loaves and the odd scraps that the priests had selected for the bag that day. Meals were a bit more regular at Aunt Kitty's.

We were outside there on a really bitter cold day. My toes were numb on the ice and the ends of my feet felt like stumps, making me walk awkwardly. The bag that came back from the priest was heavier than normal as it was passed over to Aunt Kitty. She delved inside and produced a pair of small boots. I stumbled home with her as she talked excitedly about keeping my feet off the ice and making my toes better again.

She sat me on a chair and pushed the boot over my sore toes. She wriggled it about, holding my leg with one hand and pushing the little boot with the other. It resisted her attempts. She crossed over the room and came back clutching a green bottle. She unscrewed the cap and poured a little cooking oil into each boot and smoothed it around with her fingers. Then she poured a little of the oil on my feet, after which she resumed her pushing. With difficulty, the boots finally slid onto my feet. I stood up, wobbling slightly but excitedly looking down at the first pair of boots I had ever worn. I walked uncertainly about the room for a while getting used to the strange feeling, while Aunt Kitty watched approvingly.

On the walk back to our room, I had to keep stopping and trying to ease the pressure on my crimped up toes, still tender from their exposure to the icy ground. But the oil seemed to help and my gait got steadier as I progressed, proudly looking down from time to time at my new acquisition. Mother had to help me pull them off, they were so tight. I never saw them again. She got a shilling for them.

****

I was sleeping again at Aunt Kitty's. Mother's drunken outbursts had been so bad. Aunt Kitty had settled down in her big bed and I was on a small bed on the other side of the room. The blanket was pulled up over me and I loved the warmth it gave off. I heard Aunt Kitty breathing slowly as she slept peacefully on the bed, the rhythmic noise helping to send me off into a reassuring sleep undisturbed for once by kicking feet and arms reaching out to haul the old coat from over me.

Footsteps woke me. I lay there, listening to them pad about on the lino floor. I turned and looked across to Aunt Kitty, still peacefully sleeping. I shut my eyes again. The footsteps were still there, working their way steadily across the room, from side to side. They began to come closer to my bed and I was beginning to tremble with fear. A cold breath started to waft over my face. I kept my eyes tight shut and tried hard not to move. The air kept blowing about and I sensed shapes moving about in front of my face. The bed seemed to tremble. Then the footsteps resumed, plodding about the floor for a while. Gradually they grew fainter until I could no longer hear them. Aunt Kitty stayed motionless, her bed sheets rising and falling gently with her steady breathing. My heart stopped racing and I eventually fell back into sleep.

I told Aunt Kitty in the morning.

"Oh, that's alright. You don't need to worry about her. She's no trouble. She won't hurt you. She's the white lady. Your mother came round here once to set about me. The white lady threw her out before she could get anywhere near me."

But I was not at all sure.

****

Chapter 2: Black Beetles

She was getting ready to go out for the evening, for more drinking with her cronies. Father sat dejectedly by the stove. The front two legs of his wooden chair were inside the little grate, so that he could spread his shiny hands out close to the limited heat coming from the smouldering peat. He stared at the grate, looking even more hunched than usual, with the pale evening light glistening on his bald head.

She banged about the room, shouting at us to get out of the way. Her short, stocky figure seemed to bounce about the room as she tossed things about, her large blue-grey eyes flashing us a mean stare as she caught us watching her. She dragged a comb through her tangled grey hair.

Then the row erupted. It was, as usual, hard to tell what triggered it. But she swung at father, bringing her hand down hard against the back of his lowered head. He reeled to one side, almost toppling from his chair, then steadied himself and rose to his feet. With my brothers, I quickly lay flat on the bed, grabbing one of the overcoats as a shield. The shouting and cursing grew ever louder. Their arms were waving about. Mother's punch landed squarely on his jaw, and his seemed to get her in the middle of the chest. She fell to the floor and rolled about, yelling at the top of her voice. We pulled our heads down lower and buried ourselves under the overcoats.

We could hear them still writhing about on the floor, the shouting mingled with the occasional dull thud as their fists continued to flail into each other. Eventually the noise subsided. We peered out from under our shelter. They were up again. Father, red faced and breathing hard, was standing by the stove and mother was across the room, gathering up her best coat. She shook it and swung it behind her, forcing one arm in and then the other. She straightened her ruffled hair out once again. She turned towards the window and dipped her hand into a jar kept on the sill, pulling out its contents, shaking them a little and then popping them into her mouth. She wiggled her jaw about for a moment, then headed for the door, turning as she left to yell back at my father, "I'm your lawful wedded wife and don't you ever forget it!" Dressed in Aunt Sally's coat, and armed with Aunt Sally's ill-fitting teeth, she slammed the door shut and hurried off down the stairs.

Father returned to his usual sullen, brooding silence by the fire. He said nothing as we slowly emerged from under the coats, to sit around the edge of the bed. One by one, my older brothers quietly left the room. I sat, tense and unsure, slowly swinging my legs back and forth, bumping them against the side of the bed. Father slowly turned to look at me. I sat, motionless, hardly daring to breathe. He let out a soft sigh, then slowly moved his gaze back to the grate in front of him.

I crept quietly out of the room and went out into the yard hoping to find John, the oldest of my brothers still living at home. He saw me emerge through the door way. I looked across to him, at his strong face, light wavy hair, and winning smile. He was a keen boxer and his lively energy was in sharp contrast to my weak, small frame.

"It's never going to change," he said, looking down at me. "Them," he added pointing up to our room. "It's just never going to be any different, ever."

He banged his clenched first softly against the wall. He tilted his head back and for a while stared up at the sky. Then, he looked down at me again. He bent forward.

"You mustn't tell them, but I'm getting out as soon as I can," he whispered. "I've hidden away some money. There's only one way out of here. I'm going into the British Army."

He continued to look straight into my eyes. He saw the tears begin to form, and then trickle down my cheek.

"I know, I know," he said, placing his firm hand on my shoulder. "But it's the only way."

He tightened his grip on me.

"Not one word to them, you understand, not one."

So John, the one who could stand between me and the storm, was preparing to leave, like the others before him. Suddenly, I felt the fear of the room upstairs draw tight around me again. I saw the flashing movements and heard the yelling and the screaming. I sensed the restless movement through the night and the cold air nipping at me under the old coat.

I looked up at him again. Slowly, he shook his head, reading my thoughts.

"It's the only way, only way," he said softly again.

He let go of my shoulder. He looked up towards the top of our building and repeatedly thumped his first into the wall behind him.

Lizzie, my older sister, had left long before and now lived across the city, near to Aunt Kitty, with her husband Tommy, who was away in the Irish Army. Already she had three small children of her own.

"Poor Lizzie," John would say, "struggling away with those kids, and she's not at all well herself. Needs lots of help, with Tommy not around."

When I was at Aunt Kitty's, escaping the terrors of our room, I would go to see sister Lizzie. Her home was more inviting, and had two rooms and gas lighting that sometimes worked. But Lizzie was pale now and often so weary. I would find her stretched out on the bed, the little ones huddled together in the other room.

"Can you sort them out?"

She was gasping, catching short breaths.

"I just can't move myself today."

I set about tidying the place up a bit, putting their few clothes away and cleaning out the pans under the tap in the yard outside. I filled a bucket with water and hauled it back up the stairs, placing it by the small stove in the larger room. The children could then wash their faces and sit by the warmth to dry off. I could hear Lizzie in the other room coughing and moaning, and occasionally spitting into the blue bottle she kept beside her bed.

Before leaving, I would gather the bottle and take it down into the yard, shaking out its sticky contents over the open drain. As best I could, I washed out the glass with my fingers, before returning it to her bedside. After telling the little ones to go to sleep, and looking in once more on the gasping Lizzie, I crept out and returned to Aunt Kitty's, for some bread before my long walk back across the city to home.

"Take this to you dad."

Mother handed me a small, rather battered tin. It was early morning. I thought I might be going to school. Mother's instruction declared otherwise. The tin contained a small amount of tea in one of its compartments and sugar in another, and in the middle a single piece of bread. Clutching it tightly, I headed off down the stairs and out into the streets to begin my now familiar trek across the city to the railway yard where father worked. I kept my eyes on the gutters as I went, picking up any morsels on the way, and sometimes splashing my feet around in the patches of wetness.

There were gates at the entrance to the yard, and I knew I had to wait by them until he would appear. The noises of the yard echoed off the walls on either side, the banging and sawing bouncing back between the buildings. A horn sounded off, and men emerged from the dark sheds in the yard.

They began making their way over to the gates, which were slowly swung open. Father saw me, and came in my direction. I offered up the tin, which he took in his oily hand. He dropped it into his overall pocket.

"Get along there now," he said, as he turned and headed back to the building across the yard.

I began my slow walk back home. Across the road, I saw the unmistakable figure, the portly little man in his odd pork pie hat, his leather leggings tucked into the top of his boots. I knew he had seen me. It was no use running. He strode quickly across the road and stood squarely in front of me.

"Why are you not in school today, then?" he demanded.

He peered down at me with his squinty little eyes.

"Well?"

I looked up at the enquiring Mr Dooley and selected one of the many stories I had learned to give the school inspector. He listened, a pained look spreading across his pudgy little face.

"Get yourself off to school right now," he barked, waving his arm at me.

I moved quickly away from him, looking back to see his eyes still locked in my pursuit. I turned a corner and stopped, then slipped into a narrow doorway and slumped down on the step, drawing quick breaths and wondering, once again, what might be happening in the classroom that I irregularly attended.

Eventually, feeling that I could resume the journey, I rose to my feet and worked my way through the busy streets, dodging horses and people in a hurry to be somewhere. There was no energy inside to drive me towards the school, and only a thin line stretched out before me, leading the way back home at the end of the day.

Mother went into another rage. Mr Dooley had been to our room during the day, while I had been wandering about the streets.

"Why d'you get caught by him?" she demanded, shouting at me.

"What sort of stories are you telling him to make him turn up here having a go at me?"

I pictured Mr Dooley, plump and red faced, facing the full wrath of mother, and wondered how long it had been before he made his hurried retreat. I ran from the room, with mother's angry insults echoing down the narrow stairway behind me, as I burst out into the yard and across to a sheltered corner by the wooden shed that housed the toilet. I sat, huddled on the floor, arms tucked round my knees, and looked down at my feet blacked from my day on the city streets, and as dark as my world.

Aunt Kitty offered refuge once again, but she said that Lizzie needed more help because she was not well and Tommy was away with the army for so long.

"You know, you should stay there a bit and help her out, poor soul's struggling to cope. She could do with a hand."

Lizzie said I would have to sleep in the big room as she could not fit any more into the other one. After night fell, I pulled a little mattress up in front of the stove and unfolded the sheet Lizzie had given me. I turned the oil lamp off and lay down, pulling the sheet up over me. I looked at the brown wall besides me and listened to the rasping breathing coming from Lizzie in the next room. A weak shaft of moonlight shone through the window, its grey beam cast onto the wall besides my bed. I watched it flickering on and off as clouds drifted across briefly obscuring the light.

A large black shape moved across the light on the wall. It moved rapidly upwards, passing out of the beam. Then there was another, followed quickly by more. The domed backs of countless beetles were soon scurrying across the wall besides me, glistening as the moonlight reflected off their backs. One or two would fall, landing at my bedside. I pulled the sheet tight around me, fearing that my bed would soon fill with them and that they would begin to crawl across me, making me shiver and tremble at the thought.

The moonlight finally faded. The black shapes were still just visible as they hurried up the wall besides me. I closed my eyes tight. But all I could see in my mind were the bustling black shapes, their spindly, flickering legs. I drew short little breaths and clutched hold of the sheet as tight as I could. But the image would not leave me. I rolled away from the wall, off the mattress and onto the wooden floor, hearing the small crunching sounds as my elbow struck the beetles beneath me. I leapt to my feet and headed for the door, breathing hard.

Lizzie was sleeping, breathing steadily. The children were arranged in a heap at her feet, also sleeping. I dared not climb onto the bed with them, for fear of waking everyone. In the gloom, I could see a large cloth folded at the foot of the bed. I pulled it away and hung it over my arm. Slowly, I returned to the other room. I felt my way across the floor, gingerly putting my toes forward feeling for beetles, quickly jerking my leg back if I could feel movement under my toes. Haltingly, and with my chest clamped tight in fear, I made it across the room towards my little mattress. I swung the cloth over the fender in front of the stove and held it up against the wall, securing one end behind a chair, which I pushed up against the wall. I forced the bottom edge of the sheet under the mattress, completing my barrier against the little black insects. I lay down again, my heart beating rapidly in tune with my short breaths. Every time I closed my eyes, I saw them again. I would open my eyelids and peer up at the dark clear ceiling above me, urging its stillness to guide me into sleep.

Lizzie could do less as the weeks went by. Tommy's visits were brief and infrequent. But he would leave small amounts of money for me to get food as best I could to feed the family while he was away. Lizzie coughed more as the time passed and spent many days hardly moving from her bed. She would sit up from time to time and cough up into the blue bottle, her head then flopping back down onto the bed, as she sighed and gasped for air.

Some days she could get up and then she moved slowly about the rooms, fussing over the children and doing what she could to keep the rooms tidy and neat. But she would regularly flop back into a chair, her head back, and her chest heaving steadily under her thin dress. But her pale face would break into a smile, under her watery eyes, and she would ask me once again to fetch a small glass of water for her to sip. She would stay close to the fire, her hands held out in front of her, gathering what heat they could. Then she would gently rub them together and rise awkwardly from the chair and carry on.

I made only occasional brief visits home, taking care as I crossed the city, not to be spotted during the day by the inspector. My younger brothers knew I was staying at Lizzie's and pleaded to return with me. But I said there was no room and no more food and that they had to stay at home.

"But now John's gone, we want to come with you," they piped.

I felt my heart pound in my chest. I felt the room clamp tight around me. It felt like a shield dropping uselessly to the floor at my feet.

He had gone. I saw him in my mind, all smart and strong, somewhere far away, standing proud, and free. I could see a smartly pressed uniform, the peaked cap, and a bright, glinting buckle, on the broad, shiny belt around his middle. I choked back my tears. My little brothers faces stayed cast up at mine, and I turned away.

Mother quizzed me about Aunt Kitty and what she was doing for me. She always got angry and denounced Kitty for poking her nose in where it was not welcome and for having airs about her, with her fancy hats and all.

"I'll come over there one day and give her what for," she shouted, as I headed for the door to begin yet another journey through the streets, back to my weary sister and the little children huddled at her feet.

I kept up my round of chores around her home, washing, carrying, fetching and keeping an eye on the children. But my legs often ached until I felt I could move no more. I flopped onto the mattress and lay there snatching short breaths and feeling the dullness spread through my limbs. And I choked a little, gulping for air afterwards. The room would sway gently before me and my eyes would close as I drifted into a fitful sleep.

"You should go get a little rest at Aunt Kitty's," Lizzie said,

"You look tired, doing all these little jobs for me. She's only just around the corner. We'll be alright for a bit. Go on, now."

She patted my head as I looked into her uncertain grey eyes.

I sat with Aunt Kitty as she turned the pages of the book set out in front of us. She ran her fingers along underneath the shapes on the page explaining what sound they each made. She matched the shapes to sounds and the sounds to the pictures, and I followed, occasionally glancing up into her wrinkled face. Then I stared back at the open pages in front of me.

She pushed over a sheet of paper and a pencil and began drawing some of the shapes out in front of me, making me copy the shape underneath as she guided the pencil clutched in my fingers. Slowly the page filled with the little shapes and I recited sounds as she drew her finger across each one.

"This is how you can read, you see," she said.

"You get to know the letters and the sounds they make and then they are words and that's the story."

I peered back at the open book, trying to understand the jumble of shapes, sounds and pictures.

"Mind, you would learn it better if you went back to that school like you should," she added, slowly shaking her head.

Chapter 3: Six Canes

White Friar Street School was located next door to the imposing grey priory of the same name.

On the days I went to the school, I passed by the loading bays at the Jacobs biscuit factory. Lines of grey horses stood facing the street as their carts were being loaded with the day's delivery round. Each horse had a large nose bag containing hard biscuits, to sustain it through the morning's heavy labours. I would wait to one side of the bay, watching the animals as they chomped through their meal. Some were messy eaters and the shaking of their heads would cause some of the biscuits to spill out onto the floor.

I had to be watchful not just of the loaders behind but also of the horses' powerful hooves; but if I was nimble enough, I could scoop up the fallen biscuits without being seen, and so secure some daily nourishment for myself. Some I would crunch straight away, to calm the hunger pangs in my tummy, but others I would store in my pocket for later.

School added a further welcome ingredient to my meagre diet, if, once again, I was quick enough.

There was a free supply of milk, a small bottle, one in the morning and another in the afternoon. But I had to be quick. The bottles had to be fought for, and the stronger boys were usually more successful in forcing their way to the front of the pack than I was. But with luck, most days I had some milk to drink along with the tough, dry horse biscuits.

Father Roach ruled over the school. His tall, thin and gaunt presence haunted us. The hard stare of his small grey eyes could freeze me to the spot. He stood tall before us and declared us all sinners. I sat, tired and hungry, as once again he barked out the words we all had to know, if we were going to deal with our wickedness. He drilled out the words.

"Now, all stand up," he said. "Recite with me."

He raised both his arms up and looked around the room, making sure that we were all standing.

"Hail, holy Queen, Mother of mercy, our life, our sweetness and our hope. To thee do we cry..."

His arms waved up and down as we worked our way through the recitation. As a voice tailed off, he would cast a sharp look in that direction and shout over our faltering sounds.

"Yes, yes, come on, keep up!"

We stumbled to an end. Angrily, he singled out those whose voices had fallen silent and ordered extra penances as punishment. For any or all of our little sins there was only the severest of punishment dished out by him to save our hungry souls.

I could feel the chilling sensation in the back of my neck as I knelt at the alter rail carrying out yet another prolonged penance that I had been given for the most minor of transgressions. I sensed countless pairs of eyes from behind casting a searing look, driven by speculation as to what mortal sin had brought me to this position of humbling contrition.

The recitation over, he would make me stand so that he could fire more of his questions at me.

"Who made the world?" he would demand as he towered over me. "In God, how many persons are there?"

His eyes fixed a penetrating stare as I looked up at his pinched face.

"Who is God and why does he love you so? Come on. Come on."

The questions came in torrents. To most, I knew the answers anyway, from his continuous drilling.

But when they came with such ferocity, it was all too easy to be silenced by the intimidation. And the failure to answer either correctly or at all would only produce a further torrent of his sarcasm. Every slip in my answer produced yet another penance.

In ordinary lessons, I could not sustain concentration. The words on the board blurred. The teacher's mouth was opening and closing but I was hearing little if anything. My body would sag and weaken. With arms folded on the desk lid, I would sink my head onto them, and sleep was my comforter.

Only to be jolted back to life by a whack from "Bulldog" Drummond, my teacher. His chosen instrument of torture was six canes, each split down into four strands which were then bound together at very precise intervals, so as to leave some parts of the canes exposed. This refinement meant that when they came into contact with the skin they would pinch on impact, only leaving nicks in the flesh like razor blade cuts, and not the thick weal inflicted by the usual cane. When the Bulldog punished he was not too bothered where his doctored canes landed.

The razor nicks were more painful. But they wore off quicker, often before the school day was finished. That way, evidence would not follow us home. Or, if still in evidence, could be blamed on after-school activities. Either would enable the school to avoid any blame.

But this was not so on the day of the accusation.

Father Roach appeared suddenly in the classroom.

"I have been informed that a ten shilling note has been stolen from the corner shop outside the school."

There was a moment of heavy silence.

"Stolen, you hear, stolen."

The words reverberated around the room.

"And you boy, you are the thief."

His stubby finger was pointing at me. Eyes turned in my direction. My tummy churned. My chest tightened and I drew in a short and painful breath. I stood and protested my innocence. To no avail. Father Roach removed his cold stare in my direction and slid from the room, doubtlessly devising new prolonged penances as he went. Slowly the Bulldog made his way towards me. The sea of boys parted as he made his progress across the room.

The first lash hit me across the head. I reeled to one side wincing with the pain. He pulled me up from my chair and stood me in the aisle between the desks. The next lashes were inflicted on my bare legs. The blows came in rapid succession. He grabbed my arms and placed my hands down flat on the desk lid. Moving to the side of me, he then lashed at my hands, the canes whipping into the thin flesh. He then moved behind me and deftly pulled my short pants down to expose my bare buttocks. The thin, sharp wisps of bamboo struck again and again. Their whoosh through the air providing a momentary indication of the pain I was about to feel.

In the end, I collapsed to the floor. The pain was too much to bear. I could no longer support myself. The Bulldog stood back. Sweat beads had gathered on his furrowed brow. He was breathing hard. Behind his dark brown horn-rimmed glasses, his face was flushed. For a moment the air was still and the room quiet. I lay curled on the floor, gasping in short stubby breaths, numbed by pain.

"Get up," he finally ordered, in his gruff voice.

Slowly, I pulled myself up from the floor, every muscle resisting my feeble effort. He pulled at me, dragging me to the front of the room.

"Get up here" he bellowed.

He hauled me up to stand on top of a desk in the front row, as he turned me to face the audience of my fellow pupils – somewhere amongst whom I had to assume was the real culprit of the corner-shop theft.

"Stand still."

I was to be an example he explained.

"This is what becomes of thieves."

I stood there, trembling with the pain which seared through me, from the wounds inflicted by the cane. I was humiliated in front of all the others. Exposed as a thief, wickedly stealing money from the little old lady in the shop.

But I could not be still. No will that I could summon could stop the trembling limbs still absorbing the shock that had been inflicted on them. No will at my disposal could calm the frayed nerves that caused my entire frame to tremble while I stood accused before all. I could hear the desk under me creak as my involuntary movements were carried down through it to the hard, polished wooden floor. A cold sweat sent little streams of moisture down my skinny limbs.

But the lesson continued around me. Eyes alternated from the blackboard to me and then back again. The relief of the day's first break time seemed to take for ever to arrive.

"Stay right where you are," growled the Bulldog, when the break eventually came. "Do not move a muscle."

Most of the other boys left to join the scrum for the limited milk supply. Three were instructed to stay behind to keep a watch on me. They enjoyed their charge. I knew that the slightest movement on my part, let alone any attempt to stand down from my position, would have sent any of these young conspirators scurrying to the Bulldog with fresh charges against my already stained character.

And so I remained for the rest of the morning. I hoped final relief from my humiliation might come at lunch time. But it was not to be. Once again, the room emptied. But this time the Bulldog remained in his place. Slowly, he unwrapped his sandwiches. He leant back slightly in his chair and munched slowly through the thick bread, his eyes cast in my direction as he did so. One by one the sandwiches were devoured. He slowly screwed up the paper in which they had been wrapped and let it drop into the basket beside his desk. After a while, he opened a flask and poured into a small dish what looked to me like a hot soup. Producing a spoon from his drawer he began slowly to consume it, occasionally tapping the edge of the bowl with the spoon. Once completed, he cleared away the bowl and spoon and sat, for a moment, staring at my still quivering frame. His hand slid into his coat pocket. Moments later he was tucking into an apple with hollow crunches, bite after bite.

With arms hanging limply at my side, and with the Bulldog's satisfied stare directed unwaveringly in my direction, I knew I could not risk rummaging into my pocket to retrieve what was left of the morning's cache of horse biscuits.

The light slowly faded through the course of the afternoon and I saw the occasional shaft of sunlight as it broke through casting my thinning and lengthening shadow across the polished floor. Even the shadow betrayed my little movements. I began to sway. My head was getting dizzy. I staggered. I heard a voice denouncing me.

"He's moving, sir, he's moving."

The Bulldog rose. Once again he came round his desk towards me. The lashes were directed at the back of my legs.

"Stay still boy. I did not say you could move."

But the movement was its own master by now. There was no control possible. Each movement unleashed a new beating and each beating caused more movement.

"Hail Mary full of grace, pray for us sinners now."
The words went round and round in my head. I put as much strength into my silent prayer as I could as every last particle of energy seemed to drain from me.

I prayed to God. I prayed to the Holy Mother. I prayed to the Blessed Virgin Mary. Come to my aid. Free me from this torture. Come, spread healing balm over my sore and battered body.

"Hail Mary full of grace...." As the day and the shadows lengthened, the desk grew taller and taller. Then the sound of my urgent prayer being granted rang out. The bell which marked the end of the school day. Chairs scraped, desk lids banged. Excited voices rose and feet made their hurried way to the door as the boys made their eager way home.

I turned my eyes to the Bulldog. His met mine at an instant.

"Not you," he said. "The bell does not apply to you. Stay right where you are."

"Hail Mary full of grace..." The Bulldog stared down at the exercise books as he scratched comments on the days work laid out before him. My mouth quivered. Tears streamed down my face. There was to be no end to this torture. The tears

gathered and finally dripped from my face onto the tops of my bare feet. My humiliation was complete. But the final surrender had at least been stemmed until the other boys had left. Now, no holding back. His victory was won.

And once won, it was over.

"Get down."

 The words came at me. The words I had longed to hear. But I could not move. No muscle would respond. The Bulldog rose again from his chair and came in my direction. This time he pushed me from the desk and I crumpled to the floor.

"Not just a thief, but disobedient as well. Your punishment is deserved. You'd better start preparing a full confession for Father Roach."

He continued to denounce me, declaring that only the most profound of confessions would be needed even to begin restoring my soul to a state of grace.

"Get up. Get out."

My efforts to stand were hopeless. There was no strength in my legs.

"I will count to ten."

Slowly, he began.

"One, two..."

I tried but fell back again.

"Three, four..."

The effort was in vain. The quivering legs would not take even the weight of my slight frame.

"Five, six..."

I crawled in the direction of the door. The Bulldog followed, cane in hand.

"Seven, eight..."

The door was now near. My arms were dragging me nearer with each count.

"Nine..." and his arm was raised, ready.

With one further heave I got to the door, rolled across the stone step outside and tumbled down the staircase, the banister rails lashing at my legs as I went. The sorry heap that ended at the foot of the stairs was numb through pain. The only ordeal now left before me was how to drag myself home.

Initially with only a crawl, and then eventually with a halting, limping sort of walk, I managed to get going. But I had to keep stopping. I would lean for a while against a wall. Then I could make a little more progress. Then I would sit on the edge of the road, by the gutter, leaning forward to avoid the people walking beside me. The wounds to my legs were throbbing, and I rubbed my hands over them, causing the thin layers of dried blood to drop off, releasing the moisture underneath.

I wanted there to be someone in when I finally made it home. It was mid-week, so I knew the chances of mother being there were fairly good. The money for ale would have run out by now.

I was managing with just a limp by the time I reached the corner and turned into Camden Place. Slowly I climbed the stairs and gently pushed open the door. Mother was home. And there was food. She was cooking a coddle with scraps of bacon and sausage. This was going to be the main meal of the week. There was unlikely to be more of this kind for a few days yet. Nourishment was what I needed. But it wasn't to be mine yet.

I waited, still standing. Only this time no desk beneath me. But no audience either. No attention at all. Mother pursued her rudimentary cooking. My tummy turned and my limbs ached. Eventually, father came home, his day's work done. Mother placed the stew in front of him and he tucked in. Whatever was left would be for me, my older brothers having eaten at the Bano that evening.

After my meal, mother instructed me to take the bucket, go down to the yard outside and fetch some water.   But I knew it would be beyond me now. Feebly, I said I couldn't.

"Can't do it?" mother responded.

"Can't do it?" But with rising anger now.

Father now turned towards me to await the reply. He joined in.

"Why not – what's wrong with you?"

I could not speak. I dare not speak. Father went towards his belt.   But before he could bring it towards me, my trembling hand fell to the bottom edge of my shirt. I gripped the rough linen between two fingers and slowly I lifted it and turned towards the wall, revealing the injuries to my back and legs. I let my trousers drop to the floor. All the Bulldog's work was revealed.

I stared at the peeling wall and began to shiver, not knowing whether the wait was a preparation for further punishment. Father's reaction was one of anger. It rose quickly to a rage. But this time, thankfully, not at me but about me and about what had happened. Slowly, between sobs, I recounted the day's events. I wanted him to put his arms around me. I wanted the balm of love to heal the wounds. But I knew if he did it would hurt. I wanted his hand on my shoulder. I wanted just a kiss on the head. Just anything that would soothe. Nothing came. Only a rage.

My brothers came home. They wanted to know why I was whimpering so. Father shared with them some of the story. But not my pain. That was for me to endure alone.

I was fearful of the night ahead. I knew that with my pain and injuries I was not going to be able to keep still in the bed space I shared with mother and father and my brothers. I knew that my wriggling in a vain search for comfort would result in the overcoats being dragged off the others. And I would take a further beating for being the cause of their disturbance.

The night, when it came, seemed to me like it would never end. The longer it lasted the more tortuous it became.   Here in the dead of night lay five entangled bodies, twisting and turning with arms lashing about to the accompaniment of verbal commentary,   fuelled   by   wild   dreams   and nightmares, all slowly melting into an ecstasy of sweaty human bodies – except for one, conscious of his plight, terrified of the night, fearing the morning, and now devoid of his only blissful escape – sleep.

That morning's routine was different. Father did not seem to be leaving for work at the usual time. As I thought fearfully about returning to the school, he announced that he was coming with me. As he did so, he collected a walking stick which was always kept in the corner of the room. I had only ever seen it used as a weapon. Usually when he and mother were having one of their frequent, fierce fights. He set off at a great pace and in my bare feet I struggled to keep up with him. Rage was still driving him, and I was fearful of where this morning was going to end.

After the previous day's battering and humiliation, upon my exhausted arrival the school seemed more forbidding than ever. Father halted outside the gate. I caught up and waited a short distance away from him. He held his stick part way down its shaft and swung it gently as he waited. When the other children were inside, he made his move. I maintained a distance of several paces from him, still unsure where retribution was going to be directed.

He headed for my classroom. He climbed the narrow spiral stairs which I had tumbled down the day before. He reached the door to the classroom. He peered through the small panes of glass. He raised his stick and banged on the glass, with such force I was certain it would shatter. Somehow, it held good. The Bulldog swung open the door with a flourish and lent forward across the granite step to confront the source of this disturbance. This gave father the advantage he needed. He swung his stick around, holding it at the bottom, and hooking the crook around the Bulldog's neck, he yanked it forward as hard as he could. The Bulldog lunged forward, slipped and made his descent of the stairs in a manner not dissimilar to mine of the previous day.

We followed him down, and without pausing at the bottom, father stepped over the result of his handiwork with the stick and, with me still anxiously trotting behind, made his way to the Headmaster's office. There followed a frenzied verbal exchange between the two of them. My wounds were exhibited. Cuts, bruises and discoloration were all energetically cited in the rapid exchanges that flowed on without any visible pause for breath.

Eventually the shouting subsided. Father loosened the grip on his stick. The two of them drew breath and the room became quite for a while.

"He will not need to go back to Mr Drummond's class" the Headmaster said finally.

"I think it best if I now transfer him to Mr Battersby's group."

Father moved to leave.
"By the way, we have indeed identified the boy who took the ten shilling note," the head teacher added.

"Brady was the guilty party and I have seen to it that he has been appropriately punished."

Brady. The boy whose desk I had been made to stand on by the Bulldog. The boy who had glowered up at me as I stood trembling just inches away from him. Me the example to all, elevated upon his desk. Him, the thief, slunk in his chair below, watching the blood congeal on my skin where the bamboo whipping had pierced my thin protective coating.

Brady now punished. The Bulldog laid low by father. But no relief came over me. I felt cold. My body's fight with its injuries had drained me. The lack of sleep the night before piled on to my usual exhaustion. My limbs again felt lifeless. My tummy churned once again. I coughed. The chill must have got onto my chest. I drew in a short breath and coughed again. Something sticky was in my mouth.

The dramas of the last day and night over, I fell into utter weariness. The punishment without a cause was continuing.

Chapter 4:   Not Far To Go

I had to get my feet clean, somehow. Roll call in the yard was only a few minutes away. I knew for certain that, if I was caught again with filthy feet, I would be ordered back home. I could then wash them off at the tap in the yard. I could get most of the dirt off that way. But then I would have to get back to school. And, just as before, trudge through the streets, the puddles, the gutters, past the horses, and across yards, dodging between all the people milling around me. My feet would again be in the same filthy state once back at the school.

But the stand pipe in the school yard was working on this particular morning. I had managed to get to it and squeeze my leg through to the trickling water, between the older boys who had got nearer to the source. I had managed to get both feet at least splashed with a little water and rinsed down to a presentable state.   But the older boys had then kicked into the puddles of dirty water surrounding the pipe as we left, deliberately splashing it back onto my feet. They dragged me off to the line up before there was a chance to do any further cleansing. The dirty marks ran like dried river beds across the top of my feet, the lines disappearing off between my toes.

By now we were waiting in our sorry line, and I stood at the end, hoping not to be noticed. Slowly, the teacher paced along, as if inspecting troops. It wasn't looking promising. Further down the line, I could hear him bellow out at a hapless boy. It was a case of dirty feet. He was ordered home to get clean.

'Back home.' Did he, I wondered, too go back to a small, crowded room high in the top of a brown building, with its little window encrusted with dust? There I would lie, on the days when I was just too weak to make the journey at all. There was a space on the bed now. I drew the overcoats across my body and rested my head on the bunched pillow, and breathed short gulps of air, fighting in my throat to keep the stickiness down.

I would see the light taking its daily journey from one side to the other, and hear the rain rattle onto the glass in the window. I would curl up , drawing my knees into my chest and feeling the ache inside me. Sometimes, beads of sweat dripped from my forehead, making little patches on the pillow. The long day drew out before me, my damp solitude ending only as my brothers eventually appeared around the door bustling about with their noise and filling the space around me. Days at home flattened with listlessness, punctuated by days at school, drained of enquiry.

Now, my turn. He stood before me. His eyes slowly lowered to my feet. My chest tightened up and I drew in a quick breath, and did my best to stand straight enough.

"Filthy. Can't have these feet in school, boy. Get cleaned up. Off with you."

And with that, he marched back to the centre of the yard instructing the rest to hurry off to their classrooms. I stayed put until the yard was clear, then made my way back to the standpipe. Without competing efforts for access to the cleansing water this time, I managed with my hands to clean the dirt out from between my toes. I waved each foot around in the air a little until dry. Then I slowly padded my way across the yard to the door of Mr Battersby's classroom.

I was the youngest by far. Sent here to avoid any further encounter with the Bulldog, but pitched into lessons that sailed comfortably above my head. Not that I could concentrate in any case. The words flowed from him, things appeared on his board and I saw the heads around me bend towards his waving hand like flower heads yielding to the swift air. But mine just descended into my folded arms once again as the irresistible force of sleep took hold.

Mr Battersby seemed, for a while, to accept my weary, pathetic frame in his class. For me, his was a room of some peace. A small space for me to hide away. A place where I could give in.

At times, I barely had the energy to get home at the end of the day. I could walk a little way, but then my legs would take no more, and I would crumple to the floor, and sit a while, as other legs scurried past me and the city's heart would beat around me, pushing the air across me and taking breath from me. The scene would swirl about me like scraps of paper lifted by the wind. Short little breaths sustained me while the road home lengthened into the distance. I would cough and splutter, like the grey horses lined up outside the biscuit factory.

In the room that was home, I sat cross-legged on the floor. The journey back completed, I was drained of all energy. I saw the others move about and I heard the din of talk all around me, and I saw the light of the evening fade into the dark. But it all passed by my listless body, coughing, against the wall, with its hard surface pushing into my rib cage each time I moved.

As that winter's weather began to set in, and I slumped down onto my folded arms even more frequently than before, Mr Battersby's tolerance reached its limits. He eventually summoned my reluctant mother into school.

"The boy's condition is terrible. He's always sleeping and he staggers about. He's sick. You must get him to the clinic."

We made an earlier than usual start in the morning. The direction we took on leaving home was not familiar. And I was not alone. My mother held tight onto me with one hand, and my two little brothers trailed behind. Fearful of where we were headed, I stumbled along, scraping my toes on the floor at times tearing my nails. We passed street after street, as I was pulled along, with blood beginning to trickle from a toe caught, somewhere along the way, on a split iron gutter.

The buildings seemed to lean back from the street as we hurried our way along, weaving between people and horses. I looked back, wondering where home was and where our journey was taking me. I saw my brothers slip further behind and they finally turned off down a side road, until they were out of my sight. We pressed forwards until reaching a grim, low building behind a long, low wall.

Crowds of people surrounded the entrance way. We slowly edged forward and I tried to avoid being trampled under the eager jostling. We made our way forward, slowly, eventually gaining access to the cold, whitewashed building.

We found a wooden bench and some upturned crates. I was hoisted up and propped against the wall, virtually motionless after the journey. I looked down at the floor beside me, covered with sawdust, and noticed a thick, sticky, brown line running along the edge of the floor where it joined the foot of the wall. Then up the wall there was flaking plaster work and patches of rising brown stain. The disinfectant smell caught the back of my nose as I drew in short breaths of air. The cold of the room seemed to intensify its smells and sounds. I sat, shivering, as the sounds of coughing and spitting fired through the air. I clasped my hands together.

Voices were raised from time to time, and there was shoving and pushing. People were squeezing towards one side of the room. I felt pangs of hunger surge across my tummy, recording the absence of any form of breakfast, horse biscuits or school milk.

Suddenly, I was up, being pulled across the room towards some canvass sacking suspended from the low ceiling. It was pulled to one side as we approached and I was deposited on a slippery leather surface.

"Get up" demanded the man in the white coat who stood before me.

I struggled to my feet.

"Clothes off."

I peeled off my top and trousers and stood before him for inspection. Placing one hand on my arm, he leaned forward and placed a cold disc on my chest, attached to rubber tubes, leading back to his ears. He paused, then turned casting a glance at my mother. He moved the disc around, slapping it onto me at different points. Each time, silently turning again to her.

"Turn round."

Nearly falling, I presented my back to him. Again the cold disc landed.

"Take deep breaths," he directed.

I went to draw in air, feeling only pain as I did so. I spluttered, and then made a further attempt to get the cold air into me. He continued to move his little metal disc around.

He stood back and seemed to sigh. He turned to my mother, gesturing with his arms.

"He has less than a quarter of one lung working. You must get him out of circulation straight away. He's hasn't got far to go now."

He lifted me down and passed me quickly over to mother.

"You should get him to the Pigeon House. Straight away. Next!"

As the netting was jerked back, and I was dragged forward, my feet once again shuffling through the sawdust which stuck between my toes and pinched as we made our way back to the entrance of the white clinic, its carbolic smell still haunting every breath I took.

I faced the long haul back home, with the words 'not far to go' ringing through me. I feared that my feeble, exhausted body simply would not make this journey, even with mother dragging me along by the arm. We retraced the steps of the morning, somehow eventually meeting the stairs that rose to our room. I dropped onto the bed. Mother scurried off. I slipped into another forgiving but fretful sleep.

It was hardly light when I was wakened by mother pulling at my outstretched arm. Beside her, to my surprise, was Lizzie, looking pale and tired, saying nothing, but casting a watchful eye over me as I pulled on my ragged clothes. Then, without ceremony, we set off on another journey to an unknown destiny. My simple walk to school across the muddy streets, past the horses, and through into the splashing yard played as a memory as we passed along streets I had never seen before. The buildings seemed to get smaller and thinner and the grey sky above expanded over our heads as we trekked along the open way before us.

My hesitant pace slowed even further as the surroundings grew stranger to my eyes. Mother still tugged away at one of my arms, while Lizzie's limp hand hung loosely in the other. My chest heaved and stung as the short breathes went in and out of me. In the distance, a thin black line pointed up into the sky with clouds of black swirling from its top and then bending out to one side, drifting away and thinning as it went. The air became damp and white birds whirled about glimmering against the dark sky. We trudged on, turning into a long, dark street with a low wall to one side with water stretched out beyond.

The thin line into the sky now thickened and towered above me, its wafting black smoke billowing into the air, keeping pace with the banging beat coming from below. Large carts stood in the street, piled up with coal, as the harnessed horses scuffled their hooves in the glistening black dust. My feet darkened as we passed, and spray from the water beyond the wall occasionally danced off the side of my face.

The path before us was now empty. I glanced behind, seeing the dark column stretching into the sky. The few buildings around me were low and dark. Nobody followed behind. I trod lightly on the crackling black dust under my feet.

Before us were towering black gates. I peered through the mesh stretched between the lines of iron. I could see a scatter of buildings and a yard, and little pathways leading in several directions. It seemed quiet. Barely able to stand, I took hold of the gate and pressed my face forward. Mother yanked on a large iron ring to the side of the gate and the yard echoed to the sound of a cracked bell bouncing off the walls around us.

After a while, a figure was visible. Bent, it made its way towards the black gates. I could make out a blue coat, which flapped around the legs which shuffled about beneath it. As he came near, I could make out the face of a man looking up towards us in little fits as he neared the gate. His hand grasped the iron bolt and it scraped its way from its latch. He took hold of the frame of the gate and slowly he pulled it towards him, grinding on its dry hinges. His arm rose silently as he gestured towards a wooden hut across the courtyard.

As we stepped forward, I heard again the slow grating noise followed by a clang as the gate once again slammed shut. I heard the bolt slide home, as

I turned to see the bent figure swing about and set off in our pursuit.

The wooden building before us smelt like the whitewashed building of the day before. But here no scuffling crowds around us, as mother pulled me over the low stepped entrance. Figures in hooded tops came towards me and there were soft murmurings as they looked down at me and then addressed my mother. She released my hand. I floated up into the air. Breathless I descended again onto a soft embrace. My eyes closed and mine was the new darkness all about me.

Chapter 5: Armies of Angels

It was a burning sensation that welled up inside him and moved through his body like a wave across the shore line, tugging at the grains of sand as it pulled them back to the sea bed. A wave that came again and again, with the rushing sound rippling through his head, which glistened like the sunlight dancing off the lip of the water.

The body lay motionless, only the chest wall marking out a slow beat against the passing hours. Every now and then an involuntary flicker of the eyelids as the shallow breaths crept from him.

They peered at the little body and wiped the brow with a small white cloth. Their hands gestured as fingers ran across the loops of beads and twisted about the little cross hung around their necks. They exchanged short low words with each other as they moved about the bed, flattening out the covers at its foot with the palms of their hands.

People spoke inside him without words and moved without sound. Lights came and went. Faces hollowed out before him and twisted out of shape. Then there were strange echoes in the far distance and something seemed to lift him, motionless into the air, only to fall back, slowly like a feather preened from the wing and weaving its way back down to earth.

They pressed their fingers to his little wrist and held on for a while, counting silently under their breath. They returned the hand to its place of rest, pulling over the cotton sheet and tucking its trailing edge under the mattress.

Now there was a sharpness around him and something biting at the exposed parts of his skin. A thin light caught the edge of his face placing tiny points of white on the beads of sweat that formed on the edge of his dry lips. His hair played about a little, lifting and falling as if in time with the sound of the lapping water. Droplets from the air around mingled with the moisture of his body causing small, clear rivulets to trickle onto the sheets beneath him, dappled with small black particles.

They lifted the now cold body away from its resting place and carried it back to shelter, wiping away the smuts with a grainy damp towel. They gathered the clean white sheet around him and placed his head on the plumped pillow. They drew across the thin curtain to block the sunlight from his face. They ushered the curious onlookers away and cast a protective glance in his direction, seeing the crisp sheet crinkle with the rhythm of his slowly pulsing chest.

Now it swayed and lapped around and over him, making the body splutter and causing short spasms in its thin limbs. It beat against his body sucking out the air like the retreating tide. It swayed back again and again, seemingly forced along by great beats of creamy clouds waving past and over his face. This incessant tide obeying no laws of time, just beating over and over at his defenceless shore.

They put a small spoon to his mouth containing a warm thick soup. Gently they prised their way into him, rewarded by an awkward swallow and small amounts of the fluid dribbling down from the corners of his mouth. More spoonfuls followed as the hand moved rhythmically backwards and forwards from bowl to mouth. His face was wiped at intervals, and when the effort was over more whispered words were cast over the horizontal body, before they pulled back from the bedside.

It tugged at the back of his throat and gathered in its impatience. The discomfort spread away across his chest and into his back. The little blowing sounds from his mouth deepened and became irregular. They stopped, then burst forth like rolling pebbles pulled by the tide. His chest heaved up and his head jerked to one side. In the spluttering that followed, the warmth oozed from his throat into his mouth and like lava flowed out and down the side of his face, gathering in its glistening fullness at the foot of the pillow.

They stepped forward, bent low, and with a warm, wet cloth sponged away at the mess, dropping the cloth back into a bucket from time to time and wringing it out with their pale hands. Then the dry cloth would come down and spread its fibres out across the dampened sheets and pillow, pressed firmly down and held in place. They lifted his head slightly and wiped away beneath, gently resting the cheek back onto the cotton cover. They stepped back and carried the bucket off, treading softly as they moved across the wooden floor.

The low, unvaried humming continued, with the feint clicking as the fingers moved across the small beads and the threads swung about above, dancing across the narrow beams of light that moved across his face. The cross hung before him, waving slightly, with its small arms outstretched. The air about him carried a familiar scent that ebbed and flowed in its intensity. Hooded shapes moved across in front, with glimpses of pink and cream shooting between the black shutters that flapped in the breeze.

They uttered little words of encouragement and peered at the pale face as they squeezed his hand. They stroked his bare arm and smoothed down his ruffled hair. They placed a blue bottle with a wide top on the empty cupboard set just beside the bed. They mopped and wiped and made signs to each other as they tended to the sleeping frame in the small bed positioned near the door of the wooden hut.

The sharpness was biting again. The quick stabbing pains inside kept up their tireless campaign. The air swirled about in the darkness rippling over the naked flesh lifting little bumps onto the surface and causing the body to writhe about in an effort to find shelter. Under its black canopy, the wind tricked its way about. The sea spray, cast up over the distant wall, settled onto his face as the night pulled around him, like gathering strings holding back the tugging kite.

Light shone through from the long darkness and the shadows dispersed. His pained body stirred and the eyelids drew back. A hooded figure, a cream face framed by white, leant over him. She sighed and turned.

"Mother of mercy. Come sister. I think he's awakened."

Chapter 6: A bed of my own

Gradually my senses recovered and I began to take in my surroundings at the Pigeon House. I was in a lofty, draughty room and from my bed I looked up to a pitched wooden ceiling, painted cream and supported by black iron strengthening beams that crossed from side to side of the room. I was positioned close to the door along one side of the room, with a line of beds arrayed opposite me along the other wall. At the far end of the room was a black, highly polished stove with a pipe winding its way up and into the roof.

If they stirred from their beds, the other occupants of the room would pull little wooden chairs from the bedside and gather around in front of the stove, keeping close to the mesh wire surround that hedged its way round the solitary source of heat. Occasionally, more coke would be scooped into the fire from a scuttle which stood back behind the mesh. But often the fire was not lit and the cool air would surge about the building causing its occupants to huddle as best they could under the one blanket allocated to each of the narrow beds.

The windows were small and moved outwards on little levers and seemed at all times to be open.

Even at night, when just a thin curtain was hauled across, which fluttered in the cool air. After darkness, the sole source of light in the room was a single bulb suspended on a brown flex from high in the ceiling, which gave off a dull red glow.

They were all men. Mostly old, some of whom stirred little from their beds; others rising with difficulty and shuffling about in daytime, often moving no further than from bed to wooden chair if the stove was lit. Otherwise, the only movement was at meal times. Only one or two seemed to leave the hut at regular intervals during the daytime, and often not for long.

Mostly they coughed and brought up phlegm which they spat, sometimes with success, into the blue bottles positioned beside each bed. At night, the hut would resound to a slow, discordant symphony of groans, coughs and spluttering, together with creaks from the wooden beds as they took the strain of the shuffling bodies on top.

For many weeks I continued merely to sleep, taking scant notice of the comings and goings in my new home. Often too weak to sit up and too tired to become curious, I lay, often motionless, only vaguely aware of the ministrations dealt to me by those at my bedside. My chest continued to hurt, my limbs ached and my tummy seemed never to settle. My appetite was threadbare and those attempting to feed me would melt away after brief efforts to dispose nourishment into me.

But with time, I gathered strength, and was able to sit up and take notice of those who had now entered my young life. I was attended by nuns. They were dressed in white gowns, with a stiff veil around their heads. All had large crosses hung about their necks. There was a narrow belt around their waste, with a collection of beads hanging down from the side. They rattled as they hurried about.

Many of the nuns seemed to appear on a regular basis, but there were others who would appear momentarily, casting a nervous look in my direction and then gliding off again through the doorway. I seemed to be a subject of some curiosity, the only child in a room full of men being slowly consumed by their infections. Word seemed to spread about the place and I was, for a while, the centre of attention.

The nuns kept their conversation with me to a minimum. There were words of encouragement, small instructions and regular prayers for my little soul, together with much crossing and genuflecting. A doctor came to me on occasions.

He was a fat man, with a large beak-like nose which supported a pair of little glasses, at a slight angle across his face. He would peer at me, bring a finger towards my face and lift back an eyelid. He would place the same sort of disc on my chest that the doctor had done behind the mesh curtain in the crowded building in the city. He would hold my wrist, then feel my back. He made short notes with a pencil on a little sheet of paper, which was then handed to one of the nuns. After the inspection, he turned away from me, and whispered quietly to one of them. She nodded, then looked back at me. The doctor made his way across the room to another bed, the nuns drifting along behind him.

They spoke even less if one particular nun was present. She came towards my bed and lent down across my face. I looked into her creamy smooth, pretty face and into her sparkling blue eyes. The others stood back, almost anxious in her presence.

"I am Sister Aloysius. This is my ward. I am here to make you better."

Her soft voice almost seemed to whisper at me. I could feel her breath as she bent down over me.

"You have been so poorly. But the blessed mother Mary is watching over you. She will care for you. "

She stood upright again, and ran her thin fingers through the beads hanging down at her side. She murmured quietly. She stood and stared at me for a while in an expressionless way, then gave a weak smile, bowed slightly, turned and pulled away. The others dutifully followed behind her.

I noticed one figure at the far end of my room, a bent figure of a man, who would often shuffle past the end of my bed and look in my direction without comment. I realised this was the man who had come to open the gate and who had directed my mother and I to this building, but, when, I was not sure.

My mother. My sister. They had walked with me here, I was sure about that. I remembered no parting, no words, no good-bye. I felt them now far away from me. Once again, I could see our cramped room with its solitary bed, strewn with coats, and the rickety wooden chair by the fire, with father sat, motionless and silent, his hands held out in front of the stove. And I could see Lizzie, back home with her children, waiting for Tommy, while she struggled on, now without my helping hands, somehow making her way through the long days and restless, heaving nights.

But here I had a bed of my own. And people who came to care for me.

Bridie, especially, cared for me. She did not wear the uniform of the others and she smiled a lot and when they were not around, she came to sit beside me and ask me questions. She had a soft, round face, and pale, smooth skin. Her brown hair was fastened back with a brightly coloured band that stretched across her head. She was slender, and had long, delicate fingers, that were stretched out over the edge of my sheet as she sat beside me, talking in her tuneful voice, and then smiling.

She wanted to know what I liked. She asked me how I felt. As I gained more strength, she began to tell me little stories. I listened attentively, until my eyes fell closed and her voice drifted off as I would once again succumb to sleep.

Bridie brought things for me. A wrapped sweet. Sometimes a comic. She would slip them under my bed covers and urge me to keep quiet about these treats, which were special and just for me. Bridie came to help. She told me she came from outside the city and was here to assist the Sisters in their daily tasks. Whenever she could, she came to sit lightly on the edge of my bed and talk softly about little things. She told me I was getting better, and that one day I would be strong again. She would squeeze my hand, smile at me, and plant a light kiss on my forehead. Bridie came with the daylight.

Still mostly confined to bed, I would sometimes need to be carried to the bathroom where my hands and face would be cleaned with the cold water. The simple bathroom which catered for the essential needs was at the end of the room, to the side of the stove. It had a rough wooden floor, which was stained and split. The toilet and hand wash basin were a dull white with glaze cracked with time. The basin had a bright brass tap, which eventually delivered sputters of cold water after prolonged turning of its stiff, squeaky knob.

I was then laid back into bed, and the sheet pulled up over my body. The window would be cranked fully open and the air would begin to waft about the hut.

Breakfast was porridge, ladled out with a large spoon. A cup of weak, sweet tea was placed on the little bedside cabinet. With the meal over, I would rest my head back on the pillow and listen to the sound of the whooping seagulls out over the bay beyond. Often, I would drift back to sleep, only to be awoken later by the Sisters coming to change bedding and to mop around the floor of the hut.

The stooped man returned, again clad in his blue coat. This time, he paused at the foot of my bed, lifted his head slightly and peered at me. Holding to the frame, he came to my side and again looked intently into my face.

"Getting better, yes?" he inquired.

I nodded, a little afraid to speak.

"I'm Mr Roberts."

With that he shuffled away. I watched him as he made his way to his bed in the far corner of the hut. He moved towards a collection of items gathered on a shelf and seemed to move them about, bending even more as he did so. He picked up a little item and brought it to his mouth, then returned it to the shelf where he carefully repositioned it. He slipped off his coat, folded it carefully, laid it across the foot of his bed, and levered his arched frame up onto the mattress. He cast a faint smile back in my direction.

He returned after a few days, this time sitting on the edge of my bed. He looked at me for a while, then slipped his hand into his coat pocket, producing a collection of sweets. He held them out in his hand.

"Go on, take them. They're for you. Little treat."

Cautiously, I took the sweets and secreted all but one under the blanket, while placing the other into my mouth, gently chewing at it.

"You'll like a story," he asserted, when my mouth as preoccupied with the chewing. From inside his coat pocket, he pulled forward some rolled up paper. Slowly, he unfurled it and, smiling, placed the comic down on my bed.

"Good stories," he whispered, patting the comic with the back of his wrinkled hand.

He sat back, watching me work through the sweet still rolling around on my tongue. He got up and ambled back to his corner, again carefully repositioning what I could now make out were little statues on the shelf by his bed.

I noticed that he would not be around in the mornings and was sometimes absent all day, returning only in the evening, just before lights out. He also seemed to devote great attention to the statues in his corner. That seemed to be his private space and it was never touched or disturbed by the Sisters or their helpers as they went about their daily routines.

The priest became another visitor. Father Thorne was a little tubby man, with pale hands and short, stubby fingers. His tight collar caused his neck to swell out and hang loosely down, wobbling as he spoke in his soft, murmuring voice. He seemed to attend me at my bedside with increasing regularity. He always carried his small black bible and another book of prayers. He would set them down while talking with me. He asked about me and where I was from and wanted to know what instruction I had been given during my brief, inattentive schooling.

I thought again about the angry voice of Father Roach, and felt his eyes gazing intently at me. As if he were there, right in front of me, I began reciting the words I had learned, not daring to falter as I went. Father Thorne listened, watching my lips as the words came from me. His own were moving slightly, along with mine, as if tracing the same sound.

"Well, very good now. That's very good. But there's more, you know. I can help you," he said, as I finally came to the end of my recitation.

He promised to care for me too. He said the Sisters would care for me. I told him about Bridie. He reassured me that Bridie would care for me too. His soothing manner seemed to ease a fear that had begun to grow inside me. It centred on a large man who occupied a bed half way along the other side of the room. He was often noisy, shouting and lashing out at anyone who came near him. He swore violently and stormed about the place when in a rage, banging into furniture and sometimes bumping roughly against the foot of my bed as he flailed about. When he was raging, I would flinch, and pull the sheet up over me, trying to hide away like I had to back home when mother and father were fighting.

He was tall, bulky and seemed more frightening still because of the large scarring mark that ran the full length of one of his arms.

When Bridie was at my side, he came storming across the room and demanded to know why I was receiving her attention. She did her best to calm the big brute of a man down but to little avail. He grabbed her arm and pulled her towards him. He pushed her up against the linen cupboard and pawed at her with his large hairy arms. She struggled to get free, only managing to do so by quickly slipping to her knees and crawling out from beside him as he screamed out after her. She fled from the building, leaving the large man, ruddy faced, chest heaving, swearing that he would see to her one day.

I was most fearful of him at night, thinking that he would awake in a rage and come after me as the source of Bridie's affection. When we had endured one of his stormier days, my sleep could be fitful, as I heard his groans and big heaving sighs.

Then, as a seeming deliverance, one day he was gone. His bedclothes were folded up neatly and nothing of him remained as a darkening presence in my room. Nobody spoke of him, but everyone's mood seemed lifted and faces were brighter. More people stopped by to see me. Bridie told me he had taken himself away. I was grateful that he was gone. I did not want to ask anything further.

I still had no clothes of my own and wore only thin rags in bed, cut down from grown up clothes. I never ventured far from my bed. There was still little strength in me and what there was soon drained away if I took more than a few steps. The only fresh air I knew of was that which came through the open window, or which I took in more deeply on the few occasions when I had strength to climb up on my bed and poke my head outside.

As best I could I read the comics and magazines that came my way, and listened to stories from Bridie and Mr Roberts. Stories of people they knew. Stories of faraway places. Stories so strange they whirled about in my head long after the telling. A new little world was slowly forming around me. Here, something was coming closer to me; closer than anything had before. Here was some calm and some comfort. And some food. And here, behind the heavy, locked black gates, away beyond my room, were hands that would come to take hold of mine. And promised not to leave me.

Chapter 7: The Smooth Stone

"We're going to have you up and about now," said one of the nuns.

She fluttered about my bed, her shiny face peeking out from within its white frame and her high-pitched voice piping away as she went.

"You are getting a little strength back. It will be good for you."

My long months of confinement to bed were ending. My lungs were fighting their way back to strength and my little body was beginning to experience flickers of energy. And my curiosity was increasing. At first, I was told to stay in the ward, but to get up and walk about a bit.

Some days it was still an effort and all I could do was look at my comics and peer through the window. But on better days I felt more alert and hoped people would have time to chat to me. Mostly the Sisters seemed too busy, but Bridie would always stop and talk. Mr Roberts would if he was around, but he seemed to be away from our building so much of the time, only calling back in briefly during the day to attend to his statues in the corner.

On a bright but cold day, I said to Bridie that I wanted to be outside.

"Just for a few minutes then. Don't wander too far."

I peered out from the door, and like a kitten venturing out for the first time, stepped carefully down into the yard. Ahead of me was the pathway that led to the big black gates, which I could see closed up. To the side of the gate, set low against the wall, a small building with a steeply pitched little roof and pointed windows.

On the other side of the path was a single story house, nestling behind shrubs and small trees. It looked pretty, with its painted door and little windows. Between the house and my ward were some small open-sided wooden huts, positioned on some rough ground. They had low roofs and the woodwork looked rough and splintered and reminded me of some of the buildings at the school back in the city.

I walked around the outside of my ward. For the most part the ground was stony but here and there were some little plants and patches of green. I jostled the stones on the ground with my toes, turning some over to reveal their darker side. Sometimes a little insect would scurry away as I did so, quickly concealing itself again under another stone nearby. I noticed one stone which had a little ribbon of white running through it. I picked it up and examined it closely. It felt very smooth and I ran it around between my fingers. I brushed a little dirt off its surface and tucked it into my hand, squeezing it tightly.

Back inside, I tucked the stone into a corner of the small cupboard which was next to my bed, and laid back, already tired from my brief adventure. I drifted back into sleep for a while, until awoken by a slight rocking motion and a hand on my arm. I opened my eyes to see Father Thorne peering at me.

"Sit up now. We should say a little prayer to the Blessed Virgin," he said.

I hauled myself up and clasped my hands together. He smiled a little, and holding his Bible in one hand and resting the other on the edge of my bed, he began,

"Hail, holy Queen, Mother of Mercy, our life, our sweetness, and our hope. To thee do we cry..."

He continued in his low, steady voice and I looked at his flat hand spread out beside me.

"That we may be worthy," he said imploringly.

"That's you. That's what you say," he said nodding at me.

I repeated his words.

"That's right. That's right. Very good."

He continued, prompting me to my responses from time to time. After a while he stopped.

"That's lovely. Very good, very good."

Slowly, he rose, smiled again and moved towards the door, casting me a short glance before disappearing from view.

When the nuns returned the next morning to begin their daily duties around the place, they said I should go with them.

"Just stay close by. You're going to be our little helper today."

I went with them to the next bed. They busied themselves with sheets and bottles and pans, saying nothing and going about the task with a brisk efficiency.

"Take this over to that bucket and pour it out."

She handed me a bottle containing a familiar yellow fluid, which sloshed about as I made my way unsteadily over to the far corner of the room, where I carefully poured the contents into a metal bucket. I drained the bottle and carried it back to the Sister.

She looked at it and sniffed its rim.

"No, you must rinse it out in the sink, now."

She pointed me back over to our little toilet room. I set off again with the bottle tucked under my arm. I passed Mr Roberts' statues as I went. I stopped to take a closer look. There was a colourful Virgin Mary in the middle with a small string of beads hung around her. There were other little statues of figures I did not recognise but took to be saints of some sort. It was a bright little collection, contrasting sharply with the plainness of our shared quarters.

Remembering my task, I moved on into the toilet room. I reached up to the brass tap and turned it until the water eventually gushed out. I raised the bottle and positioned it under the tap. Water quickly filed it up and it was becoming heavy. I pulled it away, jostled it from side to side and then drained out the thinly coloured water.

"Back there," she said, as I returned to the bed.

She pointed to a space on the floor where the bottle needed to be positioned.

"That's it, that's it. Now this one."

I repeated my journey, beginning my task as bottle carrier, emptier and washer. The room was now looking tidier, with all the scattered sheets removed and the bed linen straight, except where the occupants had been too weak to stir from their beds. There they stayed, curled, coughing and retching.

Sister Aloysius appeared. She came straight to me, firing a quick and sharp glance at the nuns who had been cleaning up. They stood back a little and remained very still. She took hold of my arm and we moved briskly across the room. There was a rattling of keys and within an instant I was in the darkness. I had no room to move. I was crouched awkwardly in a little space and I was gasping for air.

I did not know why I was suddenly here, and could not think of anything I had done or said that would result in such a punishment. Alone in the dark, I felt about me but found only walls. There was no way to move from where I was. I sat in my darkness. I listened. I could hear footsteps and the wooden floor creaking as people moved about. I could hear mumbling of a sort but could not make out any distinct words. I was in my darkness. There till the sounds of voices ebbed away and the shuffling footsteps were no more.

Then the sound of keys was back and the light burst in. Sister Aloysius lent forward and placed her cold hand onto my arm and pulled me forwards. Back we marched across the room, towards my bed. She bent down. Her face was like a peach, her skin shining in the day light.

 "Good," she murmured.

She turned and strode purposefully from the room pulling the door shut tight behind her. I leant into my cupboard and felt around for the little stone. I took it out and once again clasped it tight in my hand, and drifted into sleep.

I became a little more adventurous outdoors. I moved further away than the walls of my ward. Behind the steeply pitched building by the wall I found a pile of rubble. Broken pieces of brick and splinters of wood and assorted bits and pieces, rather like the little piles I had often sifted through behind the large houses in the city. I began to sift through the bits of debris as I sat, cross-legged, on the ground. There were pieces of all shapes and sizes and all very dusty and carrying a film of black on the top. My eye caught sight of something buried underneath which was brighter and looked like metal. I prised away the pieces that covered it.

Dust wafted about as I did so, getting into my eyes, making them smart. I burrowed away, intrigued by the bright little object buried amongst the rubble.

Eventually I could get my fingers through to it. I squeezed it and began to pull my hand back, scraping against the edge of the rough pieces of wood that attempted to conceal the treasure. It came out. It was a tiny model of the Virgin Mary. No bigger than my finger. I brushed away the dust as best I could and blew on it gently. It was a bright little figure. I looked at it intently, before folding it into my hand and making my way back to my bed and the cupboard at its side.

I was soon back on duty with the Sisters. By now, I was often spending the full morning with them and my duties slowly extended. I was emptying the bottles but also the spittoons and the blue bottles kept at the side of each bed. But they were hard to empty. The contents seemed solid. No rinsing under the tap would dislodge the thick sticky contents. The Sisters said they must be cleaned and gave me a stick. I poked it into the resistant substance and collected lumps on the stick by twisting it about. Withdrawing the stick, I could then scrape it on the side of a bucket, gradually shifting the dark substance from within the bottle.

Father Thorne's visits punctuated my instruction with the bottles and the pans. He asked me question about where I had been and what I had seen out around the grounds. He slowly rubbed his hands as we talked, and his neck wobbled as he nodded his head.

"You should tell me all the little places you go," he said.

He asked even more questions about what I saw and felt.

"You know there's always someone to watch over you." He nodded gently, taking hold of my arm. He listened to my little stories with a close interest.

"Now, I've something to show you." he said.

He helped me up from my bed.

"Now come with me. That's right."

We went beyond the end of my own building, along a long pathway. There was another large hut to one side and a tall red-brick building to the other, with wide gardens alongside full of plants. There were canes sticking up from the ground and in places low runs of netting with little leaves poking through. I saw some of the Sisters busy working in a corner of the garden. We turned a corner and before us sat a tin building with its wavy walls, with reddish brown marks running down from the roof. There was a little black cross attached to the apex of the roof.

"Come in and take a look."

He opened the narrow door. I stepped in and saw the blue painted walls, the rows of chairs and at the far end the bright altar with shining gold candle sticks and colourful statues. It was quiet and there was a distinct smell which seemed warming to the air. I kept looking around me. And then I looked up into Father Thorne's face.

"You can come here now and you can help me," he said.

I stepped forward and he followed me as I explored the room. He moved up to the altar and knelt before it, saying a little prayer and moving his hand forward in front of him. He motioned me to come forward and stand beside him. I gazed at the flickering candle light and its reflection on the face of the Virgin Mary who stood so firmly in the middle of the table. Her face the same peachy colour as Sister Aloysius.

Father Thorne raised himself from his kneeling position before the altar and began to busy himself with some books on a table at the side. As he did so, he would look over his shoulder momentarily, and follow my movements around the chapel. I worked my way along in between the rows of seats, running my hand over their wooden backs. I bent down and pressed my hand into a brightly coloured cushion on the floor. I came back to the centre of the room and stood, looking back at the altar and the bright, shining candle sticks.

After a while, Father Thorne walked back towards me. We left the little chapel. As we went, he promised that he would bring me back very soon.

A daily pattern was taking shape. A round of meals, helping the Sisters at the bedsides, and then exploring the grounds outside. And my strength was coming back. I coughed and spluttered less. I did not fall asleep so often. My limbs did not tire as they did before.

"Sister Aloysius says it's now time to move you," declared one of the nuns.

"So tidy away and get ready."

An instinct to gather things up quickly took hold. I reached into the cupboard at the side of my bed and removed the few comic books that were still there. I placed them on top. I reached to the back of the shelf and found my stone and my Virgin Mary. I kept hold of those. Clutching them tight in my closed fist, I sat on the edge of my bed.

Shortly, Sister Aloysius appeared. She took hold of my arm and walked me across to the door. I glanced back at my room. No faces were turned in my direction. I could see the Sisters, bent over a bed in the corner, their eyes down. The top page of my comic book fluttered open, caught by the breeze moving from the open door to the window beside what had been my bed.

We marched on, across the yard until we reached one of the open huts facing the wall and the bay beyond. There were two narrow beds. She directed me to one.

"This is where you will stay now," she said.

She let go of my arm and marched quickly off across the yard. I watched her white gown flutter in the breeze. I sat motionless on the bed, looking out across the yard towards the high wall and the black gates, locked shut. I felt the bedding beneath me, one single, thin sheet. The Virgin Mary was now digging into my clenched hand. I looked about for a cupboard but there was none. I crept out from the open side of the hut and looked down. There was a small gap between the base of the little hut and the ground beneath. I pushed my tiny statue into the gap, sealing the opening with the smooth stone. The wind from the bay came across the wall and whistled gently as it slipped through the gaps between the planks of wood that formed the back wall of my new home.

As the light slowly faded, I anticipated sleeping for the first time in this unfamiliar, open hut. Then a figure appeared. I could not recall ever having seen him before. He was quite a strong looking man, compared to the others about the place whose frames were inevitably succumbing to their fate. With little more than a mumbled greeting, he slumped onto his bed and pulled the single blanket up over him. He seemed to stare at me for a while. I averted his eyes and looked out into the blackening sky. Clouds wandered across the face of the moon and I curled myself tight under the blanket, turning my back to the penetrating wind.

Each night, back in the little open hut, it became steadily colder. The wind brought sheathes of spray over the wall from the bay, and it blew into the hut, slowly dampening my blanket which gathered ever closer to me, hugging the form of my frozen body. As I shivered, the wooden bed beneath me creaked, its thin timbers jostling against each other in an agitated fashion. Sleep was fitful at best in the grip of the freezing night.

I only saw the man at night. I never came across him during my daytime duties with the Sisters. He would not be in the hut when I returned after the last meal of the day. He would appear later. If I had

93

already managed to drift into sleep I would not see him until the morning, when, again, he would soon disappear for the day.

The night was the coldest yet. The sky was clear and the cold wind seemed more penetrating than ever. I could not sleep. I lay, shivering, fearing again the long stretch of the night ahead. Then I heard him. There were footsteps on the wooden boards. The wooden slats of the walls creaked as he made his way. I felt my narrow bed move and sag in the middle. Shuffling, he set himself down alongside me, laying his heavy arm across me. He pulled me back towards him, the full length of my body now in contact with his. I felt his warmth. The biting chill of the night slowly banished and his breathing body moved against me, feeding warmth into me. His hand moved slowly over my chest, tightening its hold from time to time. Comforted, I drifted to sleep. Warm, in my wooden hut, with the night wind cheated of its task.

He told me in the morning that this was our secret. I must not tell anyone. If I did, he would not warm me, and I would be left once again exposed to the winter night, left to shiver and tremble my way through as I had before. My warmth, safeguarded within a secret.

Chapter 8: 'Confiteor'

The first snowfall of that winter was little more than a light dusting, giving a white sheen to the ground outside but leaving all its contours intact. I still explored the grounds between performing my steadily increasing tasks.

I found a small piece of wood weathered into a nearly triangular shape, possibly by the sea or the persistent wind, or both. It was smooth along the edges that led up to its slightly rounded point. It was thicker at the base than at the top and it would stand, like a small pyramid. I kept it concealed, under the side wall of the open hut. At times I would pull it out, when I was sure no-one was looking and I would begin to pick away at the wood in the middle, pulling off tiny slithers with my nails. Eventually, I found a stick which had a sharp edge, near the pile of rubbish which had concealed my Virgin Mary. That was easier than using my fingers, and I worked away with it, pressing it into the piece of wood, opening up a space in the centre. A little came away each time I worked at it. Then I would hide it away until I could come back to it.

I had more tasks on the ward rounds. More men came in and I began to understand that they were not there for long. All struggled through their days and nights, sometimes in agony. Others were still for the most part, except when heaving up fluids of brown or red. I cleaned away at the beds and at the floor, as instructed by the Sisters.

At some beds, we stayed longer. One would stand either side and between them they would recite the words over and over again, nodding at me when it was my turn. The patient would be heaving away on the bed before us, his chest in line with my sight. I would watch it rise and fall as we went through our monotonous recitation.

"Hail Mary, full of grace. The Lord is with thee. Blessed art thou amongst women."

The man heaved again and the bed shook slightly. The Sisters momentarily looked at each other, paused, and then continued, their words gathering pace as they went.

".. blessed is the fruit of thy womb, Jesus. Holy Mary, Mother of God, pray for us sinners now."

A great sigh came from the bed. The chest went down, the bed was still.

"and at the hour of our death. Amen."

They gathered the sheet and pulled it up over the face. They made signs over the body in front of us. One of the Sisters smoothed out the sheet at the foot of the bed, as the other headed for the door. She reappeared with Sister Aloysius, who came towards me, gathered my arm and took me to the corner of the room, and with the familiar jangling of the keys that were tied around her waist, I was once again returned to my darkness.

Bundled up against my knees with my arms locked across them I waited again, still unable to understand why I had been put in here. Outside, there was some scuffling and a low voice, that of a man, I could tell. There was some scraping against the floor and more footsteps. After a while I thought I could hear another man's voice. There was more banging about followed by some groaning noises and a dull thump. Slowly the noises abated. I remained in my darkness, fearful of making even the slightest noise in this secret place.

Finally the door opened. The peachy face reappeared. She reached forward and clasped my arm, pulling me out into the room. Again, she bent down towards me.

"Good," she whispered again.

She let go of me as she pushed me gently towards the waiting Sisters, gathered by another bedside, ready once again to chant the words that had continued to echo through my mind in that dark space.

Father Thorne said there were special words I needed to learn. He sat close by me in the chapel, with the blue painted wall against his back.

"Confiteor Deo omnipotenti, "he began.

"Repeat that."

He looked down at me as I hesitantly tried to repeat words that made no sense to me but were clearly important. I had to know them. He mouthed them along with me, correcting the errors as I went. We said them together over and over.

"Now," he said, "we add these."

"..et vobis fraters, quia peccavi nimis cogitatione."

"Come on, with me."

I stumbled along the words, with Father Thorne again reshaping almost each sound as I went. The tiring lesson in this strange language ground on, numbing my mind. I wanted to be back outside, even in the cold.

"When you know it, you can go outside," he said, seeing my discomfort.

"But we have to say it some more. Until you can recite this properly."

I stayed shut in the little chapel with Father Thorne, as I tried desperately to learn the strange words he was teaching me. We sat on wooden chairs, pulled out from the front row. They were set facing each other. His wide frame completely obscured the chair he was perched on. He sat with legs apart, his hands clasped over his knees, as he lent towards me, reciting the words over and over. Finally, I was able to recite them correctly. He heaved a small sigh and rose slowly from his chair, scraping its legs back over the wooden floor.

"Alright now. That's enough for the moment. Run along. We'll do some more another day."

Freed at last from further instruction, I ran out of the chapel, past the ward I used to stay in, and over towards the little open hut where I now slept. I retrieved my piece of wood from under the hut and sat once again chipping into its centre, the small pieces which came away dropping to the floor and disappearing through the gap between the planks, falling away onto the ground underneath.

I had my secret warmth through the night. Again, we lay there bound together against the freezing night air. I felt a warm moisture on my neck. His tongue moved slowly across my skin, warming as it went. His gathering breath was at my ear. He shuffled about slightly and pressed harder against me. It seemed too tight. His hand once again slowly rubbed my chest, warming as it went. I tried to sleep but his gently rocking motion caused the bed to move about and sleep would not come until he was at last still, his breath warm against me, but his grip around me now loosened.

His arm lay limp across me. He began a gentle snoring. I pushed myself tight up against him for warmth. The strange words from the chapel began to sound again in my head. I tried to shut them out. I concentrated on the noises of the wind. It made a soft moan as it crept around the hut. I clamped my eyes tight shut, and squeezed my hands together, urging the sleep that used to take me so readily, to come again.

Mr Roberts no longer told me stories, now that I was not in the big ward. I would see him shuffling about from time to time, busy with something, and occasionally making his way over to the big gates and gesturing people towards the large building next to where I now slept. He walked past in the distance as I sat on the edge of my bed picking away at my piece of wood. He looked over, then paused.

I lowered the piece of wood onto the bed. He retraced his steps and moved in my direction. I quickly hid the wood and sharpened stick under my pillow. He was carrying something, folded over his arm. It draped down, white, vivid against his blue sleeve. He eased his bent frame down and sat on the edge of my hut. He beckoned me come down to sit beside him.

"Help me tear these up," he said.

He unfolded what I could now see were old sheets. He gripped the edge of the sheet between two fingers and bit into the cloth with his teeth, pulling the fibres apart. He then pulled hard and the sheet ripped apart as he tugged. He repeated this with another and handed it to me.

"Like this, keep pulling at it."

I pulled away and bit by bit the sheet split apart. He took the portions I had made and then bit into them again, returning them to me for yet more tearing. This way, we made four pieces out of each sheet. He took the rough torn pieces and rolled them up lengthways, making a small pile at his feet. He said little throughout, except occasional words of encouragement. When all the sheets were torn, he gathered up his pile of rags, tucked them under his arm and, with the briefest of waves, headed back in the direction of the small building with the steeply pitched roof.

Bridie still came to see me, although I did not see as much of her as I would have liked, now that I was moved to the hut, where our meetings would be more visible to anyone passing. But she brought me little things when she could and talked laughingly for just a few minutes. She would bring boiled sweets in different coloured wrappings. As I chewed on the sweet, I would smooth out the coloured paper between my fingers, trying to remove the little creases that ran in every direction across its surface. After a time, I had little pieces of various colours. All of them I flattened out with my fingers and stored them under the hut, secure under the Virgin Mary and guarded by the smooth stone.

The night air was even sharper when he came to gather me up under the blanket. I had shivered before his warmth came to me. Slowly, my trembling stopped, as he stroked my chest and again put his mouth to my neck and ear. He shuffled about a bit. He moved his hand down onto my leg, lifting it slightly. He shuffled again and then he placed something warm and hard between my legs, lowering my raised leg so that they squeezed onto him. He rocked slowly backwards and forwards, his breath blowing into my ear, chilling it where it was wet from his tongue. I felt something sticky between my legs. He rolled away from me, and levered himself out of the bed. I felt a cold piece of cloth move between my legs. He rubbed it up and down, casting it aside after a few moments. I then felt his hand rubbing the same area, smoothing into me what felt like a fine powder. He set himself down against me again, folded his arm across me and was soon snoring gently. The air around my head seemed brittle and sharp. The night had a new heaviness and I tried to get myself to sleep. But as soon as my eyes were shut, the words were there again, bouncing around in my head, with image of a brooding Father Thorne, looking pained.

"Confiteor, Confiteor..." The sounds were too jumbled. The rest of the words would not form. I knew that in the morning, I would have to try again.

He worked away patiently.

"..verbo opere et omissione."

On we went, phrase after phrase, until the sounds began to form a pattern in my head. The chapel was cold and the lesson began to remind me of the words in my school which had meant nothing to me as they poured forth from my teachers. But Father Thorne pressed on. I knew I must learn these things with him. Then I could help in the way he wanted.

With the Sisters, back in my old ward during the daytime, I worked away scraping the pans, emptying the bottles and going through the chants they made at every bedside. It left a little time during the day, during the now short daylight, for me to retrieve my treasures from under the hut and quietly work away at my piece of wood. By now there was the outline of an arch in the centre of the triangular piece. It was only shallow but it was emerging. With my sharpened stick clasped tightly between my fingers, I scraped away. Slowly, the form began to take shape.

With only thin clothes, the cold winter air pricked away at my skin. When the wind from the bay was too strong, I sat on my bed inside the hut and pulled my legs up tight against my chest. I wrapped the sheet of my bed into a roll and placed it over my feet. My cold hands made the scraping at the wood difficult. I worked in short bursts, putting the wooden block and stick down whenever I needed to tuck my hands underneath me to restore the movement in my fingers.

Now, he had moved from beside me to on top of me. His weight was crushing. The hard warmth was scraping up and down and making my back hurt. His tongue was on the back of my neck as he kept up his rocking motion, now gathering speed. He started a low grunting, which sounded like the noises some of the men made before the Sisters pulled the white sheets over them. I ran the words through my mind in case I would have to say them.

"Hail Mary, full of grace." I knew them. I could do it myself if there were no Sisters around when the time came. His grunting quickened and the bed shook beneath us. Then it suddenly stopped. He rolled off my sore back and again applied the rough cloth followed by the powder. He rolled to my side again. I heard his breathing, its pace gradually slowing until it settled into a low rhythm. I pulled my arm out from under me and felt down to my back. It was sore to touch and stung where the powder was. In the distance, I could hear the tide lapping against the shore line beyond the wall, back and forth, back and forth, in its steady rhythm. Afterwards, I waited again for the balm of sleep to come, only to see the feint light of the morning glinting in narrow streaks between the motionless bands of cloud stretched out across the sky beyond.

Bridie thought I wasn't looking well. She said she would come back later in the day to see if I was better. My back still hurt and my skin still tingled and felt sore against the rough coat that was wrapped across my shoulders. The chores were harder and I was tired. I emptied, scraped, scrubbed and folded as before and I recited but as if in a dream world. I longed for Bridie to come back, as she had promised.

"You must have a chill," she said.

She sat rubbing my hands between hers.
"They've agreed to let me get you into a hot bath," she said, "Come on."

She led me out across the yard into a building I had not entered before. We went into a small room at the side. There was a bath tub, already filled.

"Now get those things off and hop in. We've got to warm you up."

Facing me, she lifted me up over the lip of the bath. My feet dropped into the warm water and I sank down letting it lap over me.

"Ah, that's better, isn't it," she said.

She trailed one hand in the water, sloshing it about over my legs. She passed me a tablet of soap, which I squeezed with my hand and dunked into the water, causing small bubbles to froth about on the surface. Bridie chatted away and I willingly absorbed the soothing warmth of the water.

"It will be soon be Christmas. Very special."

She continued splashing the water about.

"The birthday of our Lord Jesus."

I paid little attention to her, as I felt the heat from the water seep into me.

"Come on, now, give me that soap, I'll wash your back."

I handed her the soap.

"Stand up, that's right, there now."

She moved behind me and her hand touched my shoulder. She stopped chattering. Her hand was still, then it moved a little. Then stopped again. Lightly, she moved her soapy hand down my back. I winced as she passed over my sore back. She pulled her hand away. She scooped up water and let it trickle down my back from my neck. She stopped after a while and sat me back down in the water.

Bridie's face turned to mine. She looked at me. Her eyes seemed watery and pale. She was quiet. She brought over a towel, lifted me out of the bath, stood me on the mat at the side and wrapped the towel around me.

"Now you wait here and get dry," she eventually said, her voice brittle, after a long silence.

She left me in the bathroom, sat huddled in the towel, enjoying the warmth that was still spreading all over me. Finally, she returned. She helped me back into my coat. We set off back to my hut. But we turned before we got there and made for the door of the ward I had first stayed in. Bridie opened its door.

"You are now back here," she said.

"'tis just too cold for you out there in this weather," she added, avoiding my eyes. She sat me back on the bed I had left so long ago.

"Sleep here," she said, patting my arm.

I sank my head back into the pillow, gazing at the familiar dull red light that hung down from the ceiling. My back was not as sore as it had been. I thought about my treasure beneath the hut, hoping it would all be safe until I could retrieve it.

Chapter 9: In the Dark Street

I wasn't sure about Christmas. I had heard it mentioned at home. It had happened at school. I had sensed excitement in the others there. I knew from my instruction that there had been a birth. I knew there were stories here.

Father Thorne had also told me that it was coming and that it was as special as could be and that life in the Pigeon House would be different. For a while. I listened to his explanation. He taught me more special prayers, which we recited together. I began to ask when this was going to happen. He would just smile.

"Soon, soon."

That was the only indication I got. I asked Bridie about it.

"Oh it's special, real special, you'll see."

Stronger now, I would on occasion be outside in the garden on my own. The weather was cold and I had little to shield me against the nip of the air. I sat by the shelter of the wall and imagined Christmas. Something about my days in the Pigeon House would change, I felt sure. Maybe somebody would come. There was something about someone coming. Was my mother coming, perhaps, to see me?

I wondered about Christmas when I was in my darkness again and the door was shut on me. Maybe Christmas would bring the end to this darkness. Maybe this door would not be closed on me again. Maybe all the Sisters would become kind to me. Maybe, the cold hands would not touch me.

Maybe there would be games. Two of the Sisters had started playing games with me. When I was back in my room after lunch, they would come in and lift me up.

"Stand and stretch. See how tall you can be," one would say.

I forced my arms up as far as I could. I stretched my legs.

"My, so tall."

She ran a narrow tape of paper along me from head to toe. She smiled and scribbled on a piece of paper.

"Can you catch me?" she would say, as she darted across the room, looking back at me. I chased after.

"Now, catch me, make sure I can't get away."

I ran to her and flung my arms around her to hold her and keep her from escaping.

"Now I'll catch you. Go, run."

I set off, the Sister striding after me. I tired quickly, and her arms came around me. And again she flung the tape around me. This could be a Christmas game, I thought. Breathless, I collapsed back on my bed.

"We'll play this again another day, "she said moving away towards the door, which she closed behind her with a quiet click.

The winter weather penetrated my room. A little warmth came from the simple stove in the corner which was occasionally lit. But at other times, even with a chill air swirling around the building, the windows would be open. I would lie on my bed, with the one rough blanket gathered about my chin, watching the cold air take my breath and float it away in a mist into the distance. My thin clothes were little help against the determined elements.

The Sisters were humming. They seemed to have a bit more spring in their step as they busied themselves about my ward. I asked what the song was.

"'tis a carol", she replied, "about Bethlehem, where the baby Jesus was born to our mother Mary."

I wondered about my mother. How she had dragged me to this place, through strange streets, without saying a word. I remembered us standing at the black gates, with the sound of the bell crackling through the crisp air, and everything whirling about before my eyes. I wondered if she would come at Christmas.

After many cold days and shivering nights, a Sister told me it was Christmas Eve. It was going to be a really special day. I felt the excitement grow inside me. The Sisters smiled more. They sang along as they carried out their regular duties. They said it was all going to be special for me. I just had to wait.

The girls who came in to help the Sisters were talking excitedly about presents they expected to get from their mothers and fathers. There was talk of stockings, or sweets, of pretty dresses, of shoes, and of wonderful things to eat.

But I had not seen Bridie. Did Christmas mean she was not here? That did not sound right; but where was she? Why had she not been to see me, and joked with me, and kissed me, like she always did? Surely a special time would not be one without Bridie? My worry about her cast a shadow over this rising excitement. I couldn't be really sure about Christmas. Not without Bridie.

In the evening, my room slowly emptied. Those who could, rose up from their beds, pulled on what clothes they had, and headed for the door. In the distance, I could hear the bell ringing, unusually late, in the far-off chapel. Outside, there were eager voices and ripples of laughter. I sat up on my bed, and tears began to well in my eyes and trickled down my face. I was alone again. I could see the moon, high in the night sky, past the thin curtains that had not been fully closed. The solitary moon, and me.

I lay there in the total darkness, sobbing. Unwanted. Where was the 'special' Bridie had promised me days ago?

As my sadness was wrapping itself around me, there was a sudden commotion at the door of the ward. People rushed in, some lights came on. They came to gather around me.

"Happy Christmas," they all announced.

Someone lent forward and dried my tears with a small white linen handkerchief.

"Happy Christmas".

They hugged me. The little crowd parted and I saw standing a little back from them the beaming face of my angel. Bridie stepped forward, flung her arms around me, kissed my cheek, and her soft voice whispered, "Happy Christmas" into my ear. Her tearful face met mine. I flung my arms around her.

"Happy Christmas," I replied.

Little packages then appeared on my bed, wrapped in paper and tied with string. One or two had bright coloured wrappings.

"Open them. These are our Christmas presents for you."

I leapt out from under my blanket and eagerly grasped hold of the first package I could reach. I looked up at my expectant little audience.

"Go on, see what you've got." This was special.

One by one, the little parcels revealed their contents. First, little black knitted socks. Then some cotton underwear. Then a pair of short woollen trousers. I spread my first ever new clothes around me and marvelled at their touch.

"And we have this for you."

A larger package appeared. With excitement, I pulled at the string, folded back the wrapping and gently prized open the little cardboard lid. Inside, small, black, polished shoes. I hugged Bridie again and again. Her face shone at me. Like the moon.

"Let's take a look at you with them all on then."

They began tugging the socks onto my feet and helping me climb into my pants and top. Then, as I sat with my legs swinging over the edge of my bed, Bridie knelt down in front of me and slipped the first of my shoes onto my foot. I wiggled my toes as she pulled tight the laces. Everything felt so warm. She slipped the other shoe on and tied it up.

"Now then, let's take a look at you in all your finery."

I stood, beaming, and wobbled slightly. I ran my fingers through the material of my clothes, and looked down at the reflected light on the tops of my shoes. My heart pounded with happiness.

Bridie took hold of my hand.

"We are all going to the midnight mass," she explained as she led me to the door, and out into the night air that seemed no longer cold to me.

We were a little troupe of chattering voices, working our way across the courtyard, past the wards, where, unusually, light streamed through the little windows. Once again, the sound of the bell danced through the night under the silent stars. Bridie gave my hand a little squeeze.

The inside of the chapel greeted me with a sense of magic, and with a scent I had never noticed before. There was a warmth and a glow I had not experienced at any other time in the corrugated building where I occasionally performed my little duties under the watchful eye of Father Thorne. In the candlelight, I could see that fluffy white clouds had been painted onto the normally plain blue walls. Between the clouds there were angels, with outstretched wings. I gazed about me. Faces I knew, lined and pale in their beds, looked smoother and glowed with a kindly creaminess. The normally plain altar rejoiced under more candles than usual and the gold decorations glittered sharply as the light played across their surface.

I was overwhelmed to be in this little heaven, where the joy and the happiness I felt was reflected in the dancing shadows on the walls and ceiling and in the glittering candle light.

The next day, I once again wore all of my new clothes. They seemed to give me a new energy. I explored the grounds around my ward a little more.

There were new corners and new places. I brushed aside small stones on the allotments by the wall and examined the grey earth around. I put small trophies into the pockets of my new trousers, later to be hidden about my room. Another small smooth stone, shaped by the sea across from the wall, out in the bay beyond. It had a fine ribbon of red cast through it, with another crossing over part way round. I found a small square of silver paper, creased up into a little ball. I opened it and smoothed it out. It looked like the cracked earth around me. I stowed it in my pocket. In my small world on that Christmas Day, there seemed to be more hopes than fears.

I played again in my new clothes whenever I could for more days, in between my need for rest and my duties with Father Thorne in the chapel. Each day though I played a little less. I wearied. My chest would tighten. I would cough, causing pain inside me. But my clothes comforted and reassured me in my weakness.

As I lay in bed, planning a further exploration to a yet untried corner of the grounds, my door opened and Sister Aloysius came towards my bed. She opened the small door of the wooden cupboard beside my bed and took out my carefully folded clothes.

"These are not doing you any good at all, making you rush about so."

She laid them over her arm and scooped up my shoes with her other hand. Stepping briskly, she made for the door, pulling it firmly shut behind her.

I stared at the dim glowing red light above – the everlasting light.

Chapter 10: The Wooden Arch

At first the routines were much as before. Once again, I was helper to the Sisters on their daily rounds, ministering, as the seasons passed, to the ever-changing occupants of the other beds. Mr Roberts was the only other permanent fixture, along with his shelf of saints, beads, crucifixes and his Blessed Virgin Mary.

I seemed now to spend even more time with Father Thorne. We sat together in the tin chapel as he pursued his instruction of me. Now I attended the masses as well. I would stand with him at the altar, passing him little items in the way he had trained me. He taught me to recite the words with him through the course of the service. It was often cold in the chapel, even if the air outside had warmed, and my thin clothes were no protection from the still air and I shivered, causing my voice to weaken and my responses to his prayers to drop to an inaudible whisper. He would fire a quick glance at me, and I would draw in a breath and try to make my voice a bit bigger.

He was teaching me words that sailed past me like those from my classroom. But they were important words and he insisted that I had to know them. He would take them, a few at a time, and have me repeat, over and over, until he was satisfied that I had them right.

"Regine, coeli laetrare, Alleluia. Quia quem meruisti portare, Alleluia."

I sat, hands folded, and eyes closed, and recited the sounds over and over again, looking up at the end in the hope of seeing a look of mild approval on his face. He nodded, and slowly turned over a few more of the thin pages in the black book balanced on his knee.

"I'll have you ready in time," he said, drawing to a close another of the practices which had by now become as regular as my attendance at the bedside of the suffering inhabitants in my ward.

I had retrieved my piece of wood from under the hut, where it rested without detection guarded by the smooth stone. Between instruction and sleep, I found a corner out of the wind and sat scraping away with my pointed stick. The little arch shape in the centre of the triangular block was taking shape. Soon, it would just be deep enough. I sat, working away at a corner where the wood was still resisting my efforts.

"Come on in."

The familiar voice was Bridie's. She had a small package in her hand. She held out her arm and I reached up and took hold. She levered me up from the ground. I held tight to my pieces of wood. We walked back into my ward and she sat me up on the bed. Looking quickly behind her, she opened the small package.

"Quick now, put this into your cupboard. Mind you don't wear it for a day or two though, now."

She handed me the shirt that I had unwrapped, with so much excitement that first Christmas. She beamed at me, seeing my reaction, and pointed to the cupboard. I set the shirt down on the single shelf, and returned the pieces of wood to their concealed corner. Bridie quickly patted my bed and hurried away.

The Sisters came back for further duties. One looked at me, quickly clapping her pale hands. I swung off my bed and dutifully went to her side. We moved across to a bed with another new occupant. He was leaned up against his pillow. He looked unusually sad. Seeing me, he turned and smiled, and the grey face seemed suddenly to be coloured. He lent over slightly towards me and rested his hand on my shoulder.

"Hello there, little one," he said in a soft voice.

The Sisters looked across the bed at each other and continued to adjust the sheet and to set out the pans and bottles that quickly appeared as the necessary accompaniment to all who arrived in my ward.

"I'm Mr Smith," he added quietly, patting his hand up and down on my shoulder.

The words seemed almost to choke him and he lapsed into a fit of coughing, causing the Sister quickly to swing the spittoon into position. His face was grey again. We moved on to the next bed, and I looked back at Mr Smith, still heaving into his dish, but even as he did so his head was turned slightly towards me and he seemed to be following my movements.

The Sister once again slipped into the words with ease. "Hail Mary, full of Grace." She handed me the heavy bedpan which she had pulled out from underneath the stretched out figure on the bed above. Just able to balance it, I stepped across the room to the toilet in the corner, where I emptied its contents down the bowl and, standing on the rim, reached up to yank on the rusty chain. There was the noisy gush of water as the chain jerked back up out of my hand. I took the empty pan back to where the Sisters were waiting. They were in the middle of a hushed conversation with each other. I caught only the end of it.

"I think so too. Better send for him."

One Sister scurried away, and the one who remained beckoned me on to the next bed. I looked across to Mr Smith, now calmer. I could see his chest heaving even from this distance. Again, he was looking over toward me, and he gave a little nod of his head.

The Sister returned with Sister Aloysius, who came quickly in my direction, scooping me by the arm and marching me off to the other corner, where, with the clanking of her keys, I was soon returned to my darkness. Who, I wondered, was Mr Smith? The sickly men on their beds did not, for the most part, say very much to me. I wondered how he had come here, and whether he had ever been to the whitewashed building in the city with his mother. Again I pictured his face, thinking I should go back to him as soon as I could. I sat, hunched up, thinking about the best place to have my piece of wood when it was finished. I was sure that would be soon. There were the usual voices, by now familiar to me. As they faded away, the door next to me swung back and Sister Aloysius pulled me up to my feet.

"Come with me," she said, keeping hold of my hand.

We walked briskly from my familiar ward and out across the yard over to a large brick building, entered after mounting a few steep steps. We went into a small room where there was a table and two chairs. There was a high window, the light from which fell onto the surface of the table. On the shelf under the window stood a colourful statue of the Virgin Mary. Sister Aloysius pulled out a chair and sat me down. She moved round to the other side of the table and sat on the chair opposite. Behind her on the wall hung a wooden crucifix.

Her peach face and blue eyes peered at me. She spoke very quietly.

"Tell me about the hut," she said, resting her elbows on the table and clasping her hands together in front of her. There was a moments silence as I thought back.

"Tell me," she said again, "tell me what made the marks on your back. You had bruises."

But this was a secret. I had sworn to keep it. Surely, there would be some fearful punishment for breaking my promise. Father Thorne's words echoed through my mind. Sins of my thoughts. Sins of my words. This was a new sort of agony.

She pulled open a drawer and placed a single sheet of paper flat on the desk in front of her.

"What did you see – on the man?" she added.

My head pounded and my breathing began to quicken. She pushed the pencil towards me, waving its flat end under my face. I pulled back.

"Gracious child!" she exclaimed.

She set the pencil to the paper herself. She began drawing lines on the page. Her face seemed to darken a little. She was making lots of lines, some straight, some sweeping curves. With her head lowered, she worked away with her pencil. Then, she leant back in her chair, and placing her fingers at the top corners of the white sheet, she lifted it in front of me.

"Did you see this?"

It was like my darkness again. No space to move. But the bright light from the window danced off the white page, making me squint a little as I peered at the drawing.

"Well?"

Slowly, I nodded.

"And what did he do with it? Tell me what he did with it? Come on, child."

Her voice was rising with anger now. I gripped hold of the edge of my chair and began in a soft voice, almost a whisper, to recount his closeness to me, the way his hands moved, the awkward shuffling, the breathing, the wetness on my neck and ear and the scraping of the stick – the stick of the drawing – up and down my back. I trembled as I went. Each word as it came from me chipped away at the promise like my fingers picking into my little block of wood.

"When? How often? How long for?"

Her questions shot at me like sharp rain hitting my face. I could see him and I could hear him now. I felt his arm around me drawing ever tighter across my chest. It was squeezing the breath out of me. And I could say no more. She sat looking at me from across the table. She seemed almost to pant as she spoke, but her words sailed past me.

"He shall come to judge," I could hear Father Thorne saying. In my mind I could see his black book. To judge. To judge. His face peering down at me. His eyes staring intensely. I clasped my hands tight. The room began to swirl around me. The light dimmed and then the room turned itself about and melted away from my sight.

Bridie was sat beside me when I came round. She patted my arm and smiled at me.

"There," she said looking down at me, "now mind you rest up a while. Here's some soup. I'll help you drink it."

She ladled it into my mouth and it slid slowly down my throat warming me inside as it went. The Sisters had gone and the room as quiet, but for the normal coughs and splutters. And the whoops of the seagulls high above, weaving through the grey sky.

I sat on a little chair, set to the side of Mr Smith's bed. In between coughing up into his dish, he told me a story about his days as a child in the city. How he played in the street with the others, and skipped and ran about. His story drifted along until he seemed to have no breath left. He set his head back and his chest rose and fell quickly under the sheet. His weathered arm reached out to the other side of the bed and fumbled about in a small pile of clothes folded beside his bed.

"Here," he said, summoning enough strength to speak again, "put this somewhere safe."

He pressed his hand to mine, letting a penny coin slip into my palm.

"That's it."

His head lowered again to the pillow and his eyes closed. I added his penny to the growing collection in my cupboard, tucked safely away at the back, behind the clothes that Bridie had brought.

The wood was finished after so much scratching away. And I had chosen a spot. Behind the ward, at the back wall, there was a small patch of grass, with some shrubs at one side. Mostly, it was protected from the wind from the bay and at times, when the sky was bright and the sun was out, this little corner was warm. I had all the pieces now. It could be set out.

I stood the pyramid of wood just away from the base of the building. I pushed it down as firmly as I could into the small patch of earth, to be sure it would remain securely in place. I smoothed out the ground around it and pulled away a few tufts of grass to make more space. One stone went to the left of the piece of wood and the other to the right. I set out the coloured pieces of paper in front of the stones, mixing the patterns on either side. The silver paper I folded in order to catch the sunlight and cast it up into the centre of the pyramid. I placed a fir cone against the pyramid, pushing it down into the ground to keep it steady. From my pocket, I retrieved the little statue and brushed it again with my fingers. I leant forward and positioned it in the centre of the sculptured arch, where it found protection. I drew my hands together and closed my eyes. And began my prayers to the Blessed

Virgin Mary. I implored her forgiveness for breaking my promise.

I could hear again the fierce voice of Father Roach denouncing my wickedness. I could see him standing over me, his thin face hovering above, as I wound my way rapidly through the words of penance. In my limbs I could feel again the pain of the Bulldog's lashes, as they whipped into my skin, making me flinch and cry out. I implored her to save me from more punishment. I stayed, seemingly locked in place, bent before the little arch, moving only when the pains of hunger were so great that I crept silently away.

My hands were again clasped tight before me and my eyes closed as Sister Aloysius' questions again fired into me across the table in her echoing room under its high ceiling.

"And what did you think? Did you like it? Was it nice? Did you want to do it again?"

They kept firing. My hands were clasped so tight it hurt. I was tightening all over. Even my toes were curled under my feet, so fervent were my quiet pleas to the Virgin Mary. Her drawings were on the table again, only there seemed to be more.

"Was it like this, or like this?" she insisted, pointing to shapes of different sizes.

"What happened to yours? Did it do the same?"

The interrogation ground through me. I longed to be away from it. Out in the open air.

Sister Aloysius kept drawing. She held pieces of paper up before me, and pushed them up close to me. I tried to lean back, but she rose from her chair and leant across the table, bringing herself even closer to me. Her peach face had darkened. Her eyes were tight and dark. Her voice clanging in my ears.

Finally, she fell back in silence. She stared at me from across the table. I looked down and kept fighting back the tears. I heard her gathering together all the sheets of paper. She tapped them on the table. I heard a draw slide open, and then close again. She rose, and moved across to the door. She stood holding it open, staring back at me. I pulled myself up from my chair and moved unsteadily out through the door.

I was back before my own grotto, again kneeling before her, reciting everything I could recall from Father Thorne's instruction. Even where the words were jumbled, I poured them out, faster than before and over and over until I could do no more. I opened my eyes and gazed down at her. I moved the stones around and repositioned the coloured pieces of paper, making new shapes that would please. I added some bottle tops that I had found down beside the wall that ran by the hut with the pointed roof. The bright caps caught the sunlight in this quiet corner. Sheltered by the shrubs, I was mostly out of view from those who moved about in the grounds.

I didn't even tell Mr Smith. We would talk about the stories in my comic books, and about the things Father Thorne was teaching me. I told him that I might one day sing in the little tin chapel. Mr Smith said that would be lovely and he wished he could be there to hear me. He was sure it would be beautiful. I tried to stay longer with him when I was doing the rounds with the Sisters, but they would whisk me away, saying there as work to be done. He did not complain when I left but always asked me to hurry back when I could.

I wondered if I knew enough of the words, or whether they should be said, perhaps, in a different way. But whatever I knew, I said. And added more as Father Thorne's instructions continued. I had put it together and I tended it. I wanted to spend as much time here as I could. Bridie always told me that my prayers would be answered.

Chapter 11: Two Pennies

I had asked Mr Roberts what his torn sheets were for, but he refused to say at the time. He said he would show me in due course. When I was stronger. I had not forgotten his promise. But as time passed, I began to wonder if he had. Still curious, I asked him again, now that he was sat beside me by the door of my ward. I looked up at his face, and at the prominent blue veins than ran across it and especially his nose. He sighed a little.

"Well, I'll show you," he said after a while, then falling silent again, he shuffled at the floor with his dark black shoes, making little marks in the gravel.

"I suppose it's time."

He stood up and left. The Sisters were approaching and it was time for me to resume my attentive bedside duties.

We worked our usual way round the ward, dispensing sheets and collecting bottles and pans, and I made my regular journey back and forth from the toilet, fetching and carrying, in accordance with my instructions. We came to the next bed. It was very still. The head was flat against the pillow and the chest was motionless. The Sisters were quiet. They looked closely at the grey face beneath them and one of them placed her hand under the sheet and took hold of an arm. She looked up.

"Best send for Mr Roberts", she said.

His bent figure duly appeared at the door, with the returning Sister. He carried a small bag with him, from which protruded a long wooden handle. He dropped it down to the floor and also peered intently at the calm face on the pillow.

"He's gone," he said, addressed to nobody in particular.

The Sister turned to take my arm as if to lead me away to other duties.

"No, let 'im stay. He'll help me with 'im," he said.

The Sisters left, talking to each other in a quiet whisper. Mr Roberts pulled back the white sheet. There was the bare arm, right in front of me, with heavy, grey hairs, and a long scar running almost its full length. I had seen this before and the image flashed back to me of the rough, heavy man who had pestered Bridie and who had scared me in the night. Here he was again, now laid out before me, his shrunken body unable to rant and gesture any more.

Mr Roberts dipped into his bag. He pulled out a bundle of the torn sheets. He began to roll one up tight. He handed me another, instructing me to do likewise. I rolled it as tight as I could, while watching Mr Roberts' hands work swiftly before me. He set the roll down on the edge of the bed. He placed his arms under the body and levered it onto its side. Brushing against me, he edged down the bed and hooked his arms under the thin legs, bringing them up from the knees. Then, picking up the rolled sheeting, he pushed it lengthwise into the man's bottom until just the end was hanging out.

"Pass up the handle," he said, without looking at me.

I turned to his bag and took hold of the handle. I passed it over to him. He positioned one end up against the last bit of visible sheeting and began to poke it into the man.

"Probably need another bit," he said, gesturing to the piece of sheeting I had rolled and placed on the edge of the bed.

He sent it after the first piece.

"See if you can give that a bit of a push," he said, sliding the handle down the bed towards me.

I picked it up and aimed the end towards the visible bit of sheeting. I prodded at it.

"You'll 'ave to be firmer with it."

I pushed again. The man yielded and the tail piece of sheeting disappeared into him. I pulled the handle back and set it down on the bed again, staring at the result of our work.

Mr Roberts had moved round to the other side of the bed. I could see he was busying himself with a length of string. He held it up and then bit through it with his teeth. His bent frame dropped lower still and I could hardly see him over the body between us.

" 'Ave to tie up this end an' all. Stop any leaks," I heard him say from the other side.

His face then appeared again, as he pushed the body back flat. It seemed to sigh as it resumed its position. Mr Roberts retrieved the white sheet from the foot of the bed, shook it over the body and let it settle, covering its full length and falling over the face, leaving the nose to make a small bump.

"Ready for 'is final journey now," he said.

He gathered his bits and pieces, placing them back in his bag, looked back at the sheet set out in front of him, and then he made his way back to his corner of the room and stood before his shelf of saints, speaking quietly and crossing himself over and over as he went, his bag set down at his feet, with the wooden handle pointing back at me.

Father Thorne wanted to me to sing. He hummed a tune to me and explained that the strange words I was learning with him went along with this little melody. I hummed along with him until I had it memorised. Then we went over more of the words together.

"Resurrexit, sicut dixit, Alleluia. Ora pro nobis Deum, Alleluia."

He nodded when I was finally able to repeat the sounds without error.

"You will do this for us at a very important mass that is coming," he said, "now don't go forgetting the words, will you?"

I repeated them over in my mind and nodded. I said them again as I sat in front of my Virgin Mary, adding them to the words I already knew. I hummed out the tune as I sat, once again smoothing and repositioning the pieces of coloured paper which had been disturbed by the wind.

I came back to my place when it was dark, slipping out of the ward unseen. I sat and listened. I could hear the sounds of coughing mingled with the noise of the waves lashing against the boundary wall out in the bay. The moon was full and its light caught the roofs of the buildings all around the grounds, and made reflections in some of the windows. I peered down at my Virgin Mary, shielded in her little wooden arch. I clasped my hands together again, rocking my way through all the words I could remember. And hoping that I would know them still when the important mass came.

Mr Smith did not tell me so many stories now. He still gestured to me to go and sit with him. He would smile and pat my hand. He liked me to bring over one of my comics and I would do my best to read through the story, watching his eyes flicker as I went. I would stop when his coughing was so bad that his whole body heaved, shaking the bed. Sometimes, I held the blue bottle for him, while he coughed up his sticky phlegm. When he was done, he would manage a weak smile, would breathe lots of shallow breaths and then rest his head right back on the pillow, his face pointed straight up to the ceiling. I would begin to read again, sometime adding little bits into the story as I went.

The ward rounds with the Sisters were a fixed part of my day now that my strength and energy were back. They were again busy with a man who had seemed to be in agony now for days and whose groaning throughout the night had regularly disturbed my sleep as well as that of others in the ward. He laid there now in front us, amounting to little more than a skeleton. The Sister pushed a tube into his mouth and proceeded to pour a thick brown fluid into it through a funnel edged into the top. She jostled the tube about as the fluid slid down towards his mouth. He choked and spluttered, with the brown fluid dribbling out down the side of his mouth and onto the sheet beneath him. More of the fluid was tipped into the funnel and more of it, again, ended up on the sheet. The man continued to choke until the tube was finally pulled from his mouth. Then, between coughs, he gasped for air.

Sister Aloysius appeared and there was some discussion between her and the Sisters. One of them went away, to return shortly carrying more tubing and a small bucket of steaming water, letting off the same strong odour I could recall from the whitewashed building in the city where I had once been pushed forward for inspection on the leather bench. They pulled back the sheet and turned the man onto his front, to the sounds of further groaning and spluttering. Sister Aloysius produced two leather belts and proceeded to secure each foot to the end posts of the bed frame.

She then took the tube, dipped one end of it into the steaming water in the bucket and pushed it into the man's bottom, wriggling it about as she did so. She held the other end up with her arm. She directed one of the Sisters to bring the bucket up onto the bed. And then to lift me up onto the bed beside it. The smell hit the back of my nostrils, making me cough. A funnel was stuck into the high end of the tube and I was directed, using a cup, to start pouring the foul smelling warm water from the bucket into the funnel and down the tube. The tube soon filled and water began to lap over the top of the funnel. She then passed me a rag and told me to force it into the funnel to make the water go down. The level began to drop and the man below let out screams of agony as I pushed away with the sodden rag. I kept pushing, topping up with more of the stinging water as the funnel emptied.

I stopped pushing, fearing that the screaming man beneath me would somehow explode if I went any further.

"Don't stop. Keep pushing," shouted Sister Aloysius.

After a while she leant forward and pulled the tube out of the man. She folded back the sleeve of her tunic and rolled a rubber glove along her arm. She leant over the man and began to force her hand into him. I watched, petrified, as her wrist disappeared into him. She twisted her arm about as the man howled in pain. Then, she slowly withdrew her hand, to be followed by a steady flow of what looked like small grey pebbles, which she picked up and dropped into the metal spittoon on the floor, where they bounced with a clatter.

Slowly, he subsided into a crumple on the bed. Sister Aloysius undid the belts from his feet, rolled them up and tucked them into her tunic. She told the Sisters to hurry on up with the rest of them, as it would soon be time for mass.

Still shaking inside from the images of what we had done to the man in the ward, I stood by the altar and, when instructed by Father Thorne, nervously piped out my responses. The words stumbled out hesitantly. Father Thorne glanced at me as I fell silent part way through. He waved his hand about as though hurriedly winding a clock. The image of the tube would not leave me and neither would the smell, still as strong in my nose as ever. And the poor writhing man stretched out beneath us, issuing such terrifying noises.

Peering up at Father Thorne's anxious face, I finally spluttered out the rest, "and lead all souls into heaven, especially those in most need of thy mercy." Then I sat, nervously, awaiting the end of the mass, the horrible, demanding images in my mind, punctuated only by fearsome coughing from a member of our little congregation.

As quickly as I could after the service, I made my way back to my grotto and prayed anxiously to my Virgin Mary to forgive me for the pain I had caused the poor man in the ward, and to plead that I would not be made to do it again. I knelt until my knees were numb on the damp ground underneath me, then went back inside and waited hopefully for waves of sleep to wash over my head.

He was still the next morning and I desperately wanted to avoid having to do anything to him or even see him on my rounds with the Sisters. I was still consumed with guilt for the things we had done to him and fearful of any punishment that might come my way, even from his enfeebled body. Fortunately, he seemed to remain asleep as we carried out the usual chores around him. I wondered if Mr Smith had seen what had happened and whether he would say anything to me about what I had done. But he too slept through our ministrations, his shallow breaths whistling quietly as they left him.

Mr Roberts said that our work from earlier was not all finished and he wanted me to come with him. We crossed the yard outside and headed towards the small building with the steep roof, which I had seen but never yet entered. It had two small doors.

He took out a key from his coat and wrestled for a while with a lock. It seemed to take a long time before it clicked open, and he pulled up a little handle and levered open the first of the two doors. He gestured for me to enter. The inside was lit by just two candles so it seemed very gloomy despite its little windows.

There was not much space between the tables set out along the room. One was empty, the other was covered with a shape concealed under a white sheet.

"Here, this is what we do," said Mr Roberts, as he began folding back the white sheet, causing the candles to flicker in the wafting air.

He looked over the body, easing it up gently and checking underneath. He dabbed away a little with a cloth he produced from his coat.

"Seems about right," he said, looking down at me. He placed his hand into one of the pockets of his blue coat and produced two pennies which he showed me.

"Look at this, "he said, "watch carefully now."

I levered myself up as best I could, standing on tip-toe. Once again I noticed the long scar running the length of the still arm resting just inches from my fingers. Slowly, he placed each penny over an eye, making sure they would not slide about. He made sure I had seen this operation take place, then nodded for me to stand back a bit. He slowly unfurled the white sheet again, all the way up over the body, tucking the edge underneath to prevent it hanging down from the side of the table.

With his cloth, he turned and began wiping down the top of the empty table, taking care to cover every square inch. When he had finished, he motioned to me that we should leave, and as we went, he placed the latch down on the door and once again wrestled with the key. As I stood watching, I noticed a cart leaning up against the side of the building. It was a simple creation, with plain planks and what looked like pram wheels. It was a bigger version of the one I had once wheeled around the city streets gathering scraps of food, at a time that now seemed far back in the past. Mr Roberts was done. It was time to leave the little morgue and its sole occupant, resting peacefully under its white sheet.

I thought again about the man opposite, now still, but who not so long ago had screamed in pain at the things we had done to him. And about Mr Smith too, who had said nothing, but who had, I was sure, seen what went on.

Chapter 12: Solo

"You will be doing your little song for us next Sunday," said Father Thorne, after we had concluded another mass in the tin chapel.

The long months of rehearsal were over. After the last person had shuffled from the building, he placed a hand on my shoulder.

"Just sing it through for me now, one more time."

Nervously, I began and, concentrating hard, got through all the sounds I had been going over in my mind for what now seemed like an eternity.

"There, lovely," he murmured, patting my head. "Off you go now."

Bridie explained Easter. She had told me about Christmas each time it came around. Easter, she now explained, was about living again. She said that was what my little song was about, and that it was in special words because it was a special time. She said she would be there to hear me sing. I thought about all the people who had come to the Pigeon House since that day, long ago, when I had arrived and how all of them had died, and how Mr

Roberts and I had prepared them for their final journey. And I wondered if they were all now living again, somewhere in the city.

Once again, I sat cross-legged in front of my private grotto, quietly asking the Virgin Mary about all those who had departed this place during my time here. There was a rustling in the shrubs beside me, causing me to jump. No-one had ever come to be with me when I was in this place. I was afraid that if I was found here, my wooden shrine would be taken away. I sat very still. And then again, the rustling, and small, whispering voices. I wondered if I should run and hide, but I wasn't sure where. And something compelled me to stay.

The rustling continued a little way off. Slowly, I turned towards the source of the noise and looked up. Through the leaves, I could see shapes moving about. But they were dark and small. Then one of the figures pushed its way into and through the bushes. It came through to stand before me, quickly followed by another. I looked in disbelief, unable to understand why they were here. My little brothers. My heart suddenly raced and I thought I must be imagining things. The two figures I had last seen, looking back over my shoulder, so long ago, turning off into another road, as mother had dragged me along to this place. Now they stood here before me, bare foot and ragged.

"Got any food?"

Their first words of greeting to my astonished ears. But without answering I simply rushed forward with a string of questions about how they got here, how they got in, how did they find me.

They explained their long walk from the city and their search for this place, how they had scaled the wall and crept carefully around the grounds avoiding being seen by anyone. Again, they complained of their hunger. There had been no food at home for some time, and they said that they had little choice but to try to seek me out. They had heard that people here were given regular food. I had little on me, or in my cupboard, other than a few sweets. But I had an idea.

Leaving my brothers with strict instructions to stay exactly where they were, I set off across the grounds towards the building where I knew food was prepared for the evening meal. I reached the building and crept around it. Its door was shut but there was an open window at the back. I reached up and placed my hands on the sill of the window. I lodged one foot onto the space between the planks of the wooden wall and levered myself up. Pulling hard, I was able to get my head through the open window, far enough to get a good look round. There was food there, ready for that evening's meal. Squeezing myself through, I dropped down inside and made my way across to the table. I stuffed bread rolls into my pocket and scooped up vegetable leaves in my hands. Climbing back out, I made my way back to my brothers without detection.

We spread our little feast out on the ground and they quickly devoured it, talking excitedly between mouthfuls, every now and then hushing ourselves for fear of detection.

My brothers were a little bigger now, changed in some respects from when I had last seen them on the day I was brought to the Pigeon House. They talked of their life – my old life. Nothing had changed. Like me, they begged, they went hungry a lot of the time, and they had nothing really to wear.

They too only attended school irregularly. It seemed to me they were treading a path I knew well, but which now seemed so far back. I told them about the bed of my own, and about the meals. I told them about Bridie.

As I talked, I felt the eyes of Father Thorne on me, and I saw myself back in front of Sister Aloysius undergoing more terrifying interrogation. I felt the pull back towards my hungry brothers. But also felt again the misery of their world. And I wondered if there was another way.

We talked until the light began to fade. We waited until it was almost dark before working out a route by which they could escape with the least chance of being seen. We worked our way, staying close to the ground, over towards the little house where Father Thorne lived. Hurrying across to the bushes at the side of the building, we stopped there to recover our breath. It was time for them to scale the wall and to begin their trek back, through the night, to the city beyond, and to another room, up at the top of narrow stairs.

I imagined walking back with them, through the dark streets, but to where? I did not know where they would be going. They had moved so many times, from room to room, as before. They were going back to a life no different than before, their days numbered still by hunger, arguments, fights, hiding, begging, but also by playing, and laughing.

Where did I belong now? Should I scale this wall with them? I saw Bridie's face. I saw Mr Smith, flat, grey, tired, but turning to me and smiling. I saw Father Thorne, urging me along with my now well prepared song. And I saw Sister Aloysius, and suddenly felt fear sweep over me. I would be found. They would bring me back. And the punishment for fleeing would be hard to imagine. I looked up and saw their feet disappearing above me. Their legs swung up over the top of the wall. Their faces momentarily appeared, glancing back down at me. Then just darkness. I, back here by myself, by the side of my wall. They, somewhere on the other side, no longer hungry, tramping through the black dust in search of the way home. My legs felt slow and heavy as I trudged my way back to my bed.

"Now, I'm coming along to hear you sing to us today," said Bridie, after she had finished the next morning's duties around the ward.

There were a few more faces dotted about the little chapel as we eventually got under way. Father Thorne seemed to have more to say than normal and the service stretched out before me, as I kept running the sounds through my head. Then, he gestured me forward from my customary position at the side of the table. He hummed a little note, and then the room fell silent. I could see Bridie, towards the back, and I could see Sister Aloysius in the front, her gaze cast firmly towards me. I took in a breath, and launched off:

"*Regina coeli laetrare, Alleluia. Quia quem meruisti portare, Alleluia....*"

All the faces were on me. I saw them all but now saw no-one. I strained away at the sounds and the notes, pausing slightly for breath at points, and then pushing the words out, just as I had time and again cross-legged on the floor in front of my little grotto.

I reached the final 'Alleluia', and stopped. I could see the faces again. Bridie's beaming from the back. Father Thorne was speaking again, and there were murmurings from around the room. He waved his arm a little and I stepped back to the side of the table, my heart pumping and my clasped hands moist and trembling.

Mr Smith had not been there. For days now, as I tended to his needs with the Sisters, he had stirred little. Only coughed. Such words as he exchanged with me were issued between quick breaths. I wanted to tell him about my song. I went to his bed side and looked up at his face. His eyes were closed and I could see his chest rising and falling quickly underneath the sheet. I stayed a while and presently his eyes flickered open. He saw me, and a weak smile came across his face. I began to tell him about my song. I said I think it was pretty, as people had said it would be. In a low, hoarse voice, he said he was sure it had been. And he wished he could have been there to hear it for himself. His eyes closed again and he gasped a little more for breath. I turned away and left him, glad that he knew I had managed to sing it all on my own, at a special mass.

Sister Aloysius reappeared. Once again, looking quickly behind her, she took me by the arm and we crossed over the ward to the far corner. Without speaking, she undid the door and pushed me forward into my darkness. The door slammed shut in front of me and the clanking noises beyond were followed by the sound of footsteps on the wooden floor, heading away from me, and then by the voices.

What were my brothers doing now? I wished they could have heard my song. I wondered if they were once again hungry. And if they would ever return to see me. The noises beyond continued. The same chattering that always seemed to happen, the mix of a man's voice amongst that of several women. But I could make out no particular words. I listened to it continue, until eventually there were footsteps again, slowly quietening until all I could hear was the coughing in the ward. Then the door opened and I was pulled back into the light. Sister Aloysius guided me back to my corner of the room, and then let go of my arm. She peered back at me. I wondered if she would say anything about my song. But she said nothing. She moved away, once more glancing back before she disappeared from view beyond the door.

Bridie came to me as I climbed back into bed, preparing for the night. She said my song had been lovely and she hoped one day I would sing again in a special mass. She patted my hand, wished me good night and I watched her as she went around the ward, checking on everyone, smoothing out sheets, tidying, and making sure pans and bottles were where they should be. The last lights went out, save for the ever-glowing red bulb suspended from the ceiling, and in the gloom of the night, she walked softly from the room, giving a little wave in my direction as she went. I lay back, pleased that she had heard me and that she hoped to hear me again. I looked up at the red glow, which slowly dimmed from my view.

There was a rustling sound. The leaves and branches of the shrubs were moving. Hands appeared inside the bush. The noises came again. The hands flicked before me, but no faces came. Had they come back? I felt myself moving as if the ground beneath me were lifting me higher. Then I dropped back down again.

My eyes opened. There was the dim glow of the red light. I lay still. The rustling sound came again. Then I saw from the corner of my eye the whiteness. I quickly shut my eyes again, and felt my chest tighten. I waited. Slowly, I opened my eyes again. The whiteness was still there, visible in the strange glow of the night. I dared not look in its direction. I lay as still as I could. But the sheet around me was moving. I could see it, a little way down from me, rising and rippling. The white figure bent a little closer to me. Then I felt a hand fall gently onto my leg. I clasped my fingers tight. The hand was still there. I realised the white lady had found me. She had left Aunt Kitty and the city. She must have wandered the streets for so long in search of me. And now she had found me. And Aunt Kitty was not here, with me. She could not come across and make the white lady go away.

I dared not move and prayed hard to the Virgin Mary that she would make the white lady go away instead. But the hand did not go. It moved upwards along my leg, sending shivers through me as it went. The fingers moved across towards the middle and reached out beginning to stroke me in the same place that the man in the hut had stroked me, when we shared our secret warmth. The fingers stroked, then squeezed. They pulled at the end. Then squeezed again. My heart pounded and the nails of my fingers began to cut into the palms of my clenched hands.

Strange movements began inside me and I felt my rigid body stiffen even further. The hand moved slowly backwards and forwards, squeezing momentarily as it did so. I tried to hold my breath but couldn't. I let it out slowly, despite wanting to gasp. My heart pounded in my chest. The stroking fingers spread over me, making the sheet rustle as it rose and fell in time with the hand beneath. I held my eyes clenched tight shut, for fear of seeing her. I wished I could rush to my grotto and fall to my knees before the Virgin Mary. But no force would move me, as I lay frozen, rigid on my bed.

Then I felt a sharp pain and my legs jerked, followed by my whole body. The hand slid quickly away from me and the sheet once again settled down over me. There was more rustling at my side, followed by a waft of the night air across my face. The barely audible sound of muffled footsteps was followed by the creaking of the door and then the drop of its little latch. I lay motionless, breathing rapidly. Slowly, I opened my eyes again, seeing only the red glowing bulb. I turned to my side and peered into the darkness, seeing nothing. I listened, hearing only the breathing of the others and the rasping sounds in their throats. She had gone.

I shuffled uncomfortably, trying to make the stinging stop. But it continued with a beating rhythm, slowing slightly as my breathing began to resume its normal pace. Where had she come from and why had she left the city and why had she come for me? Why, if I had sung so nicely, as Bridie said? Why, as I had not left with my brothers? Why did she want to hurt me now? My fears held me awake through the night.

After the dawn had broken, the Sisters returned to set about their first duties of the morning. I watched them as they hurried about. They came to Mr Smith's bed and paused. I saw them take hold of his wrist, raised up from its resting place on the bed. The Sister held it for a while, then lowered it back into place, looking at the other as she did so and slowly shaking her head. She took hold of the white sheet and unfurled the edge, raising it up over his face and letting it drop down again, tucking the end under the pillow as she did so. Together they stood at either side of the bed, and in turn, mumbled the words which were by now so familiar to me. I said them in my head in time with them.

"Eternal rest grant him. Let perpetual light shine upon him. From the gates of hell deliver him."

They cleared away the pans and bottles from the side of his bed and withdrew. The light from the morning sun cast a beam across the white sheet stretched over him. Tiny specks of dust drifted across the beam, bright for a few seconds, then again suddenly invisible.

Chapter 13: Lying with the Dead

So now Mr Smith had passed away, like the others. Another turn in the regular cycle at the Pigeon House. Another step along my daily routine. Just like any of the others, I worked on him, preparing him for his exit from the Pigeon House. In the way that all exited, having succumbed.

Mr Roberts and I were told by the Sisters to get him over to the mortuary as quickly as possible. It was likely that someone was coming into the ward to see another patient, and it would not have been right for there to be a dead body present.

"Get this sheet over 'im lad," said Mr Roberts. "We got to get 'im out to shed quick as."

We spread the white sheet out over his corpse, folding the loose edges under the body and tucking them in as best we could. Mr Smith was probably better dressed than he had ever been. With one of the Sisters standing by obviously impatient to see his remains removed, we needed to work quickly.

"Fetch in the cart, " directed Mr Roberts.

We had a simple cart with a crude wooden base and two rather uncertain wheels. The contraption was tied to two long, rough handles. This was the means by which the final journey from the Pigeon House would begin.

The cart was jerked into position alongside the iron bed. There was some height difference. With Mr Roberts taking the head, and me stretching up as best I could to get my hands around his feet, we heaved Mr Smith from bed to board, and adjusted the white sheet as best we could, to keep every inch of his deceased frame under wraps.

Then we began the journey out from the ward, across the rough ground to the mortuary positioned close to the front gate. The wheels jostled over the step outside the hut. Mr Smith rolled a little from side to side. We reached more level ground. But after moving from the side of the hut into more open ground, we were suddenly exposed to the fierce wind blowing off the bay.

It flapped at the white sheet and tugged at its folded corners. I pushed the cart along from behind with one hand and tried to secure the sheet with the other. But the wind was swirling about as if to the tune of a Death March. There was rain in the wind and droplets were blowing straight into my face as I tugged and pushed into the wind. Bent as he was, Mr Roberts worked from one side, and me from the other.

But the gale was winning. The sheet flapped more and more. It billowed as the wind found a willing opening. Suddenly, it lifted from one corner, whipped off the body and blew back to cover me. I could see nothing. The sheet howled about my face. It sounded as if I was in a collapsing tent. I flailed about with my arms trying to find a way out from under my white world. I managed to grasp a flapping corner and pulled it towards me. I could poke my head out at last to see where we were headed.

"Get it back over 'im", I heard Mr Roberts yell over the howling gale.

I tucked the lively edges of the sheet under the body as best I could. We resumed our halting progress towards the mortuary. A continuing battle between the rushing air striking out its own song and our feeble efforts to move the last remains of Mr Smith.

Finally we reached the little mortuary building with ourselves just upright and Mr Smith still horizontal. Mr Roberts struggled with the lock, rusted under the battering of so many years of salty sea spray. As the playful wind continued to tug at Mr Smith's final covering, Mr Roberts got the lock open and pulled back the first of the two little doors that opened into the final resting place for the residents of the Pigeon House.

The cart would not go through until the second door was open. It had to be opened into the wind. Mr Roberts set his hunched back against the partly open door and gestured to me to push the cart through. With what effort I could muster I heaved away, willing the little cart over the small but stubborn final wooden step. With relief I felt the cart jerk forward and, bumping roughly against the partly open second door, our charge reached his destination.

The door slammed shut behind us. The sheet was still. The body in place. The wind whistled through the narrow cracks between the planks of wood that made up the sides of the mortuary. The roof creaked in sympathy. And the two candles that stood alight on the small table at the other end of the room flickered uncertainly as the wind darted its way through the dark little building.

"Up onto slab," instructed Mr Roberts.

Taking our respective ends, we heaved Mr Smith from wooden cart to cold mottled grey marble. At first, he made it just to the edge. I pushed him a little further, sure that he would then be centred and appropriately composed. All told, three residents of the Pigeon House now lay still together, their struggle over. Their remains occasionally sighed gently as they waited in the dank space in the weather-beaten little hut.

Mr Roberts leaned against the slab, breathless after his efforts. The still open door banged back and forth, its metal latch crunching into the wood frame as it hit.

"Best lock up and get back," said Mr Roberts. Checking that the two candles had survived the assault of the gale, we left. Mr Roberts did not bolt the door. He just swung the metal lever across leaving the latch up.

"Can't be fidlin' with that in this wind," he said as he shuffled away back to the ward, with me following in his meandering stride.

Back in my hut, I was now alone. The bunk opposite me, where Mr Smith had laid, was empty, with a rough woollen blanket folded neatly and placed at its foot. The stained pillow, now without any case, sat at its head. The wind maintained its whistling joust with the timbers of my little home. Through the wind I shortly heard the clanking of the bell summoning us to the evening prayers that preceded the final meal of the day. I levered myself off my bed and slowly made my way across the courtyard and on up to the chapel, glancing as I went at the hut where my roommate lay.

My eyes darted around the chapel. Low figures around me mumbled though the prayers, bent before the altar, coughing and spluttering as they trudged their way through the words that formed such conversation as many had during their time in the Pigeon House.

"Glory be to the Father, to the Son and the Holy Spirit, as it was in the beginning..."

Was Mr Smith moving to glory I wondered? His time here was done. He was heading...somewhere. But was he leaving or had he may be already left the Pigeon House? I wondered where he was and where he was going, and how he would get there.

"hail, holy Queen, Mother of mercy, our life, our sweetness and our hope. To thee do we cry, poor banished children of Eve..."

Light bells rang out and the nuns sang in a brittle voice, competing with the gushing wind outside. My tummy rumbled and my head felt light. I desperately wanted the food that was shortly to be consumed. And I wanted something or somebody to come and soothe me. I yearned for a companion. A true companion. One who would stay with me and one who would look out for me.

One who would be like Bridie, but who would stay with me and not disappear. Perhaps be with me through the squally night ahead, so that I would no longer be alone.

"Lead our souls into heaven especially those in most need of thy mercy." Amen.

We trouped our weary way back to the ward where the food was served. We ate mostly in silence, with just a little murmuring, in company to that of the wind through the eves – and the coughing that punctuated all time in the Pigeon House. The Rosary rounded off our meal as usual.

"...who was crucified, dead and buried..."

I walked sluggishly back to my now lonely ward and sat on the edge of my bed. I prayed for Mr Smith. I wanted Mother Mary to ensure he was now safe, and that he would find sweetness and a little hope. He may have found some sweetness in his time with me, but he was moved away. Far away from me. I shivered.

Dead, but not buried. I wondered more about Mr Smith. I lay back on my bed, watching the dim, single red bulb as it swayed gently above me, after lights out. I had my little red glow to watch over me. Like Mr Smith's candles.

"He shall come to judge the living and the dead."

Mr Smith would be judged. We would all be judged. But we should be ready for our judgement. I wondered if Mr Smith's sheet was still in place, or whether the cruel wind had found its way into the mortuary and disrobed him again, lying there in his final nakedness, being judged. I looked across the bed where he had laid and felt a kind of loss.

Despite the exertions of the day, sleep would not come. I pictured Mr Smith. Maybe we hadn't done everything we should. Maybe in the haste we had overlooked something important. Maybe he was not ready for judgement.

I sat up, and swung my bare legs over the edge of the bed, letting the tips of my toes rest on the cold floor. Slowly I edged myself forward and stood facing the door, the faint light casting the weakest of shadows before me. I stepped slowly towards the door, reached up and lifted the latch. I pulled the door back and peered out into the damp night. I looked across to the little mortuary. Something seemed to be calling me over.

When I reached the building, I gently levered up the latch, remembering that Mr Roberts had not finally secured the door as usual. The small door creaked open and I stepped in. Mr Smith's candles were flickering. But their light was so poor, I could not tell whether his sheet was intact or not. I took a few paces further towards his slab. I stretched out one arm to feel for the edge of him, using the other to distance me from the body which I knew lay to the side of him.

With a loud bang, the little door slammed shut behind me, caught in a powerful gust of wind. I heard the 'clack' of the latch as the force of the action pinged it loose. One of the candles darkened and then expired. My heart pounded. I could see nothing. I could only breathe the scent of death, and hear the laughing wind.

I cast my left hand about in the dark. It came to rest on his cold foot. Working my way up his leg, I moved forward, but standing as far back from the slab as I could without losing contact. My right shoulder brushed against the body to his side. I knew I was moving up the narrow isle between them, towards the table at the top of the room. The one remaining candle fought against the darkness, providing my sole guiding light.

My heart beat faster still, almost in time with the flicker of the dim candle. A sense of panic overwhelmed me. Maybe I should not be here. This was a fear I had not felt before. It was turning me cold with beads of sweat dripping from my brow and freezing on my face as my limbs gradually became fixed through my bare feet to the cold stone floor.

The wind disturbed the shrubbery outside the morgue, causing its stiff branches to scratch angrily against the wooden panels of the building. Now I had joined Mr Smith. I was his companion again. Locked together with him. Perhaps he would take my fear away. I edged towards the top of him. In the faltering light from the candle I could see the edge of the white sheet. On tip-toe, I reached out and caught hold of it. Slowly, I peeled it back.

First, some wispy hair appeared, then the domed forehead and then the full face. Expressionless. Still. The cold eyes staring to nowhere. We had forgotten something. With horror, I realised we had not placed the pennies over his eyes. I gasped with fear of our mistake. This was not how Mr Smith should be.

"He shall come to judge the living and the dead."

But surely not like this. I wondered if there was anything I could do to complete the task we had failed to do. Anything I could do to be fair now to Mr Smith. Another fierce gust of wind shook the building and the slight compression of air snuffed out the last remaining candle. I could no longer see his opened eyes. And I wondered if he lay there baring me ill will for all the things I had done and left undone.

More than anything else I wanted to get out of the mortuary. But I was frozen with fear. The door had slammed, the candles were out. All I could do was feel my way about but I was petrified of what I might touch as I did so. My bare feet were cold on the stone floor and I was shivering, not certain whether this was the chill or my dread of being there. Cautiously, I finally extended an arm to grope about. At first nothing. Only the chilled air. I stretched a little further. There was the cold flesh I knew I would meet. I pulled my hand back with a jerk. There was nothing for it but to sink to the floor.

Slowly, I knelt, until my knees touched the ground. I knew I would be unable to stand for much longer. Feeling out around me, I eventually lowered my whole body to the floor and curled up into myself.

My mind danced about. Visions of the dead mingled with visions of devils and purgatory. I kept seeing Mr Smith's staring eyes. I saw us again packing his body ready for its departure to this place. I heard the intoning voices of priests declaring on sin and punishment. The sounds and the sights all whirled about in my mind.

My night dragged on with the terror in my head deepening as it went. Against the hurling wind outside I knew no-one would hear me if I cried out. There would not be anyone about in any event. And I was certain it would be wrong to make such a noise in this place. Here I would be until somehow and by somebody I was found. And I shook with fear at the thought of what punishment would then come my way, for being here in the first place. I waited, breathing quick but shallow gasps of air, accompanied all night by the ghosts of those who had died in my sight and whose frail bodies I had helped prepare for the final journey in their mortal existence.

Some had been nice to me. They had smiled at me, patted my head, slipped me a sweet or a penny. They had sat with me, and sometimes held my hand. They had given a kindly word, or two. Good ghosts. Jostling for space with those who had scowled at me, sworn, pushed me away and made fun of me. Tormented demons. This congregation of ghosts seemed to squabble over me even now, their echoing voices flitting over my head like bats in flight.

The intensifying cold was now too much to bear. I reached up and waved my hand about until it found the edge of the sheet covering Mr Smith. I clung to it for a while and then, with a tug, pulled it as hard as I could. It came rustling down to the floor and I quickly gathered it towards me and tucked it around my trembling body. I bunched one corner of it as best I could and lay my head on the little mound. It was musty and damp but it was a comfort still, as I faced the long, stretching night ahead.

After a while, I shifted myself to ease the numbness in my legs. I lifted myself up slightly and lent my back against the wooden leg supporting the slab above me. A demon struck out at me. A cold weight slapped into the side of my face. I took in breath as a shudder went through me and locked myself into place with rigid fear. It stayed there, as if clinging to me. I slowly raised my arm towards my face, until it came into contact with the cold surface of a hand, hanging down limply from above. In taking his sheet for my protection, I had caused Mr Smith's arm to topple off from the side of the slab above and it was now hanging down limply beside me. My sins deepened.

A thin blade of light appeared under the door and I heard the sound of birds. The morning had at last come. Now I yearned for rescue while fearing what consequence my mistaken journey would have. I thought I should attempt escape before I was found. Now there was enough light to guide me, I crept down to the door. It would not open. The lock had certainly slipped into place, as I had feared. Some light was visible between the rough planks that made up the door and I edged my fingers into the narrow gap. Maybe it would be possible to force a gap just wide enough for me to crawl through.

I picked away at the narrow space, digging my nails into the frayed edge of the wood. Tiny shards would come away on one side where the wood was damp and rotting. But the next plank was tough and my nails snapped as I tried to pick into this stubborn defence against my freedom. I kept trying, the tiny splinters digging into the ends of my fingers and causing them to bleed. The gap was barely big enough to poke a finger through. I would surely be found before I could make an escape.

I realised that there would be tell-tale signs of my misdeed. My morning routine was not to be carried out on this day. So there would be no crisp altar cloth laid out in the chapel and the priest's prepared vestments would be nowhere to be seen. Things done and things left undone would now surely find me out.

Morning gathered itself slowly. I began to hear the usual sounds of the Pigeon House preparing itself for another day. I heard doors open and close. I heard mumbled voices in the far distance. And coughing. Then footsteps, which gradually grew louder, until they stopped on the other side of the wooden door. Then the jangling of keys and clank of metal. The door swung back and the sudden stream of daylight caused me to recoil, knocking my head against the wooden leg of the frame behind me.

"Holy Mother, child," exclaimed Father Thorne.

He looked down at the crumpled heap before him. He grabbed my arm and pulled me up, causing me to wince with pain. He gathered up the sheet from the floor and shook it vigorously. I jerked my head over to one side to prevent it whipping into my face. He cast it up over Mr Smith and it slowly settled across him, assuming his shape. Father Thorne grasped his dangling arm and levered it back under the repositioned sheet.

He lent forward, his face coming to within inches of my own. His breath wafted across my face as I studied the deep veins on his nose. He brought his rough hands down onto my shoulders.

"Holy Mother," he repeated, tossing his head from side to side.

He let go and stepped beyond me. He moved towards the far end of the mortuary and arranged things on the low table. He re-lit the candles. Facing the far end of the room, he began to mutter.

"Requiem aeternam dona eis, Domine,"

He turned and looked back at me, slowly shaking his head from side to side. He lowered his head to one side, giving a slight gesture with the back of his hand. He turned away from me again.

"et lux perpetua luceat eis."

He turned again, and, as if, under his breath, said,

"Here, come up here."

I stepped forward. He handed me a small dog-eared piece of white card, withdrawn from between the pages of his black book. The printed shapes I recognised. He carried on with his mass. I whispered the responses I had learned each time he cast a pained look down in my direction.

He splashed holy water about the room and the hurried little mass was over. The undertaker had arrived and stood at the open doorway. Father Thorne nodded at him and gestured him in. He was followed by a further tall, thin man. They set a plain wooden coffin up on little trestles and hoisted the body of one of my night time companions into it. They fastened on a lid. Neither of them gave me even a glance. They hoisted the coffin outside.

Father Thorne brought his hand to the back of my head and propelled me forward, out of the mortuary and into the searing strong light of the morning.

Chapter 14: The Black Shoe

The punishment began with a cold bath. Sister Aloysius stood like a statue, her arms folded beneath her shimmering cloak as she watched me climb reluctantly into the tub, and dip my foot down into the icy water. I glanced back at her. There was not even a flicker from her face. She kept her gaze locked firmly on my flesh. Slowly, I slid down into the water, goose bumps forming all over my arms and chest. I sat, letting the cold grip take hold of me. I grasped the sides of the tub, trying to lever as much of me as I could out of the biting water.

She stepped forward, rolled up her sleeve, and dropped her hand down into the water. She began to splash it about, lifting it in streams above me and dropping it onto my shoulders and down my back. I tensed up under the impact, but she continued to pour the water over me, without uttering a word. I felt the water reaching out all over me and gripping my shivering body, refusing to let go.

Rising to her feet, she finally stood back, looking down at me. She dried her hands on a towel, set it over the back of a wooden chair and left. I waited. Confident that the punishment was over, I climbed out and hastily wrapped myself in the towel, trying to stop the shivering. I rubbed the towel over me, still moving carefully over the sore and still tender areas. Wrapped in the towel, I returned to my building and to my bed. Bridie saw me come back. She came across carrying a large grey bottle. She lifted my sheet and slid the bottle up close to my skin. I felt its warmth spread out and embrace me.

"I'll fetch some porridge," she whispered, and returned shortly with a pleasingly warm bowl. "I'll be taking good care of you," she said, as she tucked the sheet close to my thawing body.

Later, when I felt warm again, I slipped out of my bed and returned to my hidden corner in the grounds, and to my grotto. I tidied it and once again carefully rearranged the stones and the paper. I picked up the statue and blew away the dust that had settled on it. I replaced it firmly inside its protective shelter, pulling away the little blades of grass which had sprouted across its front. Fervently, I begged forgiveness, and asked that Bridie would be alright and that she would, as she had promised, be able to look out for me.

I could not sleep. I crept out into the grounds and sat in my secret corner, often gazing up at the sky and listening out for the sounds of the bay. As I looked up at the stars above, I heard the lapping of the water against the stones beyond the wall. I breathed in the familiar scent of the sulphured air, mingled with that of the rotting seaweed on the bank beyond the wall. My mind raced about, leaping from images of the sick, to their pained faces, and then to their still motionless bodies. I heard again the voices of the sisters as they sped through their words at the bedside. There was Mr Roberts, bent over, working away on the bodies, with me at his side. And there too was Father Thorne, reciting, urging my responses, and bringing me again to his altar table. There again was the running water out in the bay, splashing against its shore line and then draining away, the little pebbles rattling as it went. I thought about the wall my brothers had scaled that night. I wondered what was down on the other side and what would happen to me if I was there, on the other side of the big black gates. I clasped my arms together around my knees and rocked myself gently in front of the little statue.

After a while, I returned to my bed, hoping that sleep would now come. I lay still, watching the dull red glow in the roof, and hearing the sounds of the night through the open window, and the sounds of the taught throats fighting for air all about me.

I heard the door opening. A soft footfall moved across the floor towards me. It stopped beside me. With my heart thumping, I prized open an eye just enough to make out the white shape beside me.

There was the rustling noise again. The white shape lowered, sinking onto its knees. Small hands, emerging from the ends of the whiteness, came together, their fingers enfolded. I opened my eyelids a fraction further. Head bowed, and lips moving slightly, Sister Aloysius prayed at my bedside.

I strained to hear her words, while closing my eyes tight shut. I could not make them out. Then I felt the hand move onto the side of my leg, stroking up and down. Then it began to push at me, forcing my leg up. Her hand then slid quickly underneath me, her finger resting over my bottom where it circled around the rough skin. Slowly, she forced her finger into me. A pain shot through me and I wanted to scream out. But I feared what she would do if I did, so I stifled my cry. Her other arm now lay across me and she lowered the hand across my front, once again stroking me and pinching my skin, pulling it back until it stung again. I clenched my teeth together and tried to steady my breathing. There was more pain. Her hand let go of me and then clamped down over my mouth, making it hard to breathe. Her finger worked backwards and forward inside me and the pain shot through me in waves, the tide rushing into my ears, with a thumping hum.

Until, as I gasped for air, her hands withdrew and I rolled onto my back, where I could see in the gloom her peach face glowering down at me, her dark eyes staring intently into mine. She stood motionless, our gazes locked by some irresistible force. Then, she swung around, and headed for the door, the red glow catching the back of her white robe as she went. I felt the tears well in my eyes and then trickle down my face onto the bed. I wiped my eyes with my fingers and then placed the wetness against my sore skin, hoping to ease the pain.

The Sisters chided me and demanded me to get up and help. Bridie also wondered why I was not getting up. She rolled back the sheet and took hold of my hand.

"Come on now, you cannot be staying there all day."

I levered myself to the side of the bed and sat up.

I heard Bridie gasp, and I turned to look at her face. It was white and her eyes were fixed, staring down. I looked down too. At the blood stained sheet. Her hands trembling, she ushered me across to the bathroom. She brought in a jug of hot water and poured it into the sink. She gave me a cloth and told me to wash myself down. She left, saying there was something she must do. I should carry on cleaning myself up. She would be back to see me when her urgent task was completed.

I kept my pain to myself. The Sisters hurried about their business. Mr Roberts was not there, and would, I thought, by now, surely know about my break into his morgue. He would probably also want to punish me. And Mr Smith was gone. And Father Thorne too would still recall his early morning discovery. I could only return to my space, to the little grotto, curl up, and hope nobody would come to find me. And there I slept, the sun on the back of my neck in a warming caress.

"What have you been saying?"

I was back in Sister Aloysius's little room, where she had made the drawings and fired so many questions to me about the man in the hut.

"What? What?" she demanded, her eyes flaring.

"Telling nasty little stories?"

Her face lowered close to the table as she looked across directly at me.

"Wicked, wicked!" she shouted out.

After pausing, she rose from her chair, and came round to my side of the table. She pinched my ear between her fingers and jerked me upright. Still holding onto me, she sat down again, and pulled me across her lap. She jerked my shorts down. The slaps came down hard, like the Bulldog's cane. And they stung. She slapped over and over again until my skin felt raw. Then she stopped, breathing heavily, looking down at my whimpering frame stretched across her knee.

I felt her lean away, with one arm still holding onto me. I heard something thump onto the table above me. Then her hand again landed on my bottom, only this time softly. And it was moist. She began to smooth her hand across my skin, spreading the cream about. It was cold and smarted against the raw surface of my skin. Then I felt something warmer, wet, moving across me. I strained my head round to look back. I could see her head bent down and her face pressed against me. Her tongue moved about across my skin, going from side to side and down in between my legs. I drew in short sharp breaths as she moved over me. Below me, I could see her black shoe, quivering slightly, the shine causing the light to swim about as it moved.

Her hand kept sliding over me. Then her fingers were pushing away in between my legs, moving backward and forward over me. Then she circled the rough skin in the middle and began to push her finger into me. I winced as a pain shot through me. Her arm clasped me tighter as my body shook.

She withdrew her finger, and hauled me off her knee. I could barely stand on my shaking legs. She threw my rags at me and ordered me to get dressed again.

I ran back to my room, the pain still thumping into me, and asked for Bridie. Nobody had seen her. She had not been back. When the Sisters returned in the evening, she did not come with them. I asked where she was and when she was coming.

"Now don't go bothering yourself," came the reply. "You have your work to do. Now hurry yourself."

I carried the bottles and washed them out. The Sisters passed things to me without uttering a word. I went through the now familiar routines, until, at last, they parted, closing the door quietly behind them.

I lay down but no sleep would come. I lay awake anxiously awaiting the creak of the door. Every little sound made me jump. The wooden building would respond to the rush of the wind in the night, and my heart would leap. Or when the rain came, and lashed the windows like tiny pebbles, I would jump in fright. The noises from the others echoed harshly through the air.

Morning would creep in but I would remain in darkness. It followed me through the day, through my chores around the ward and through my responses in the tin chapel, and it was with me when Mr Roberts and I were preparing more bodies for their final journey. It lay over me like a suffocating blanket, blocking out air and light. It hung around me still when I was knelt before the grotto, pleading forgiveness and mercy. And asking why Bridie did not come to me anymore.

Chapter 15: The Narrow Gap

"Again, say it again."

She sat at my side, making me endlessly repeat the words of confession. No day went by since she had begun coming to me in the night, when Sister Aloysius did not stand over me, demanding the words from my lips.

"I confess to Almighty God," I began over again, "and to you my brothers and sisters."

The words were echoing through me as I spoke,

"that I have sinned through my own fault."

I looked up at her. "Go on, go on."

 "In my thoughts and in my words," I continued, as her relentless stare drilled into me.

Then the Sisters burst into the room, waving frantically at Sister Aloysius. The recitation stopped. She pulled my arm and marched me off again to the darkness in the corner, while the familiar voices began their chattering on the other side of the door, once again shut against me. Only this time, the light shone through a little. Puzzled at the difference, I leant out and rested the palm of my hand on the inside of the door. It shifted. I pulled my hand back quickly. Through the narrow gap, I could see the huddle of figures gathered around one of the beds. There was Sister Aloysius, two other Sisters and, with his back to me, a tall figure of a man in a white coat.

Again I nudged the door a little and it opened further. In the haste to bundle me away, the latch had not been shut securely. Prompted by my urging, the door slowly opened on its hinges. I cast my eyes about the familiar room. The figures around the bed continued their earnest discussion. I was not going to stay put. The open door was its own invitation. I stepped out and after a momentary pause, began to walk across the room, back to my corner.

One of the Sisters was in mid flow when she saw me. She stopped immediately, causing the others to look at her and then follow her eyes. They turned. Sister Aloysius' face froze. The tall man turned. He looked like the man in the whitewashed building in the city who had sent me here.

"Who is this?" he demanded, turning back to the Sisters.

"What is he doing here?"

183

They all turned towards Sister Aloysius. She remained frozen, her face pale and taught. He motioned me to come over towards him. I moved forwards cautiously, uncertain of what reaction would come from any of the Sisters all of whom now watched my every move, transfixed. He pulled out a chair and lifted me up to stand on it. He lifted off my jumper and proceeded to plant his metal disc on my chest. First one place, then another. He turned me round on the chair. The disc landed on my back. He handed me my jumper. He turned to the Sisters.

"Boy's perfectly sound. No business here at all." How long has he been here?"

One of the Sisters could contain herself no longer.

"I think about three years. He came..."

She was cut short by Sister Aloysius.

"Now Sister, I can explain, doctor."

A testy exchange took place between them, the doctor's face darkening as Sister Aloysius picked her way through a story I could not follow and which seemed to my ears to make no sense at all. Finally, he stopped her.

"Well, he's got to be taken out of here, just got to be. Totally wrong. Get his family here to take him home."

He looked at me again, without saying anything more, and shook his head. The Sisters averted my eyes and stared intensely at the floor in front of them.

'Family, home'. The words rang like bells in my head. Was this happening to me? I stood back from the group and began to walk slowly over to my bed. I kept checking that the doctor was there, knowing somehow that I was safe while he was in the room, but fearing that some terrible retribution would befall me once he was gone.

When his work at the bedside was done, he turned to leave, the Sisters following close in his wake.

"To be out of here, you understand. Gone before I have to visit again."

And then I saw the last wave of his white coat as he stepped out of the room.

Silently, and slowly, she crossed the floor towards me. Her arm stretched out and roughly took hold of mine. She dragged me once again across the floor to the bathroom, where she slammed the door shut, and proceeded to fill the metal tub with cold water. She ordered me to undress and get into the tub and sit down. Again, she rolled her sleeve and scooped up the water in order to drain it down my back and over my head. She moved rapidly about the little room, fetching more water and throwing it about, splashing some of it out onto the floor. She drew heavier and heavier breaths and dropping the bucket she had been using to sluice me, she began banging her clenched fist into the palm of her other hand, making a smacking noise that bounced around the little room and which made me squint in fear each time it came. Finally, she stormed from the room, banging the door closed behind her, leaving me trembling in the freezing water, listening to the drips from my hair splash back into the slowly swaying water in the tub.

I clambered out and hastily wrapped myself in the towel and dried off my shivering body. I crept back to my bed and dragged the sheet across me, burying my head in the pillow and wishing that Bridie would come again with her warming bottle. I stayed stretched out on my bed, slowly recovering from the plunge into the cold water, until darkness fell outside. The Sisters returned shuffling about the ward in their duties, but not expecting my assistance. None of them spoke to me as they passed by the foot of my bed. They left, leaving me with only the abiding groans and coughs for company into the night.

Then the door swung open again. Sister Aloysius marched across towards me. I flinched as she approached. She reached her arm down under my head and forced me into an upright position. She held her hand behind my neck and forced my head forward. I held my eyes tight shut in fear of what was to come. Then I felt something hot against my lips, forcing at my mouth. She pulled at my jaw, and my burning lips parted. She thrust my head back and held the hot glass firmly against my face. The searing, cutting fluid swilled into my mouth, and I choked as it slid down my throat. I spluttered and writhed about, trying to break free of her firm grip. But she pressed the glass harder into my face, with her other hand pressing into the back of my head. The hot liquid tore at the back of my throat again. I could see her face now, towering over me, distorted by rage. The hot fluid had splashed over her white robe, making dark stained patches stand out against the brightness of the material. The intense pain inside me swelled and I felt my muscles clamp, then loosen. The urine flowed out of me in a seemingly uncontrollable manner, quickly spreading a warm moisture right cross the sheet beneath me. The glass pressed into my face was now empty. She drew it away, throwing it onto the foot of the bed. I dropped back onto the pillow, my insides twisting and burning.

Then she yanked the sheet and empty glass away and forced me over onto my front. My stomach pressed down into the wet bed and my face was squashed into the pillow. Then her sticky hands were on me, smearing a cream of some manner all over me. With her finger, she pushed some of the cream up into me and it immediately caused an intense burning inside. She leant down, her face coming up alongside mine.

"If you ever breathe a single word. A single word, you hear. I'll be back with more."

With my face pressed into the pillow, the words jostled in my head. My insides rolled about and I writhed on the bed in agony, unaware for a while that she had left, and I was there, flat on the bed, under the glowing red light, feeling the dampness spread about underneath me.

With difficulty, I dragged myself across the room to the toilet, where the pain underneath grew yet more intense as my insides seem to shoot out from underneath me. I gripped the sides of the bowl for support as the room swirled about me and the knives twisted ever more deeply in my tummy.

Out in the ward, I could hear someone crying out for help, as happened so often in the night. But I could not move in response. I dare not move, fearing that I would crumple to the floor the moment I attempted to stand. Even if I could, and was found back in the room again, I feared that it would bring only more punishments from Sister Aloysius. I gripped on tighter still, expecting that I would never reach the day the doctor had decreed for my release from this place. I panicked at the thought. I knew for certain that I must not die in the Pigeon House. I knew that my battered and sore body would only have to endure even greater assaults if I did. I was determined not to let that happen.

I dared not leave the bathroom until light had broken outside. I knew then that others would come and that I needed to be out before that happened. Easing myself forward, I stood uncertainly, the pain and discomfort still tearing at me. Steadying myself against the wall, and against items of furniture, I crept back to my bed. I longed for Bridie to come. To feel her warm hand in mine. I could tell Bridie. She would understand. She would comfort me. She could cool the burning heat that still pulsed inside me. But she did not come.

When the Sisters came, they looked at me, and at my sorry bed, and said I had a bad bug. That meant no breakfast, only sips of water. The others were told to keep away for fear of catching it from me. I was left in bed, with gulps of water charged with quelling the fire that burned inside.

It was days before I could move about with any comfort and before I could face taking food as before. But once able to move about again, the Sisters pressed me back into their service, passing me the bed pans and the bottles to empty, and the soaking cloths with which to clean up the soiled mess left around and on the patients whose insides had, like mine had just done, given up any semblance of control. Sister Aloysius stood over me, to ensure that every duty was performed exactly as she willed it. The Sisters avoided her stare and busied themselves, maintaining their lowered heads.

Every day, I peered out towards the big black gates, hoping to see them open, and familiar faces appear ready to stretch out their hand towards me. Again and again, they remained shut.

It was a bright morning and I was beginning to feel recovered from the ordeal of a few days before. As I finished my breakfast and anticipated joining the morning's ward round, one of the Sisters came over to stand beside me.

"Now, pack up your things. You are going home."

I began to pull my few belongings together. There were some shorts and a woollen jersey and some socks and the pair of black shoes that had been given to me that first Christmas at the Pigeon House. I reached into the back of my cupboard and felt around for the collection of pennies, which had grown as small gifts had been pressed into my hand by Mr Smith and by some of the girls who came in to help around the ward. I split the pile into two and dropped equal amounts into the pockets of my shorts, their weight hanging down in the lining. One of the Sisters collected my other clothes together and wrapped them in brown paper, neatly tying off the little package with string, looped into a large bow big enough to slip my hand through.

"Come now, this way."

The Sister held out her hand and took mine. I picked up my parcel and together we headed out of my ward for the last time. I looked back towards the corner behind the building where I had put together my little grotto. I slipped my hand free and made to head off towards it. The Sister quickly reached out for me, grabbing hold of me tight.

"No. No. You can't. Come along, there's no time . You have to go."

Across the yard, I saw Mr Roberts emerging from the morgue. I looked across at his drooped figure and saw him begin to make towards the big black gates at the far end of the yard. From the other side, I could see Sister Aloysius approaching, her bright white robe dazzling in the morning sunlight. She too made towards the gates. The gates I could still hear banging closed behind me and which I had come to believe would never again open for me.

We were now drawing closer to them. I could see a figure waiting by them, just on the inside, and I could see that one gate had been pulled back a little way to let her in. Mr Roberts and Sister Aloysius reached the gates ahead of us. I saw them standing alongside the little figure. Mr Roberts looked bent almost double, standing beside Sister Aloysius. As we approached them, he moved forward, cutting across in front of the others. He stood before me. For the very first time, I held out my hand towards him. He hesitated, then moved his towards me. I took hold of his rough hand and squeezed it with mine. I looked up into his face, and saw tears well in the corners of his eyes and begin to wend their way down across his lined face. In his other hand, he held a large rusty key, which was swinging on a small chain, causing a black shadow to sway across the front of Sister Aloysius's white gown as she stood a little back behind him.

Her eyes followed me, imparting their unspoken warning, as I stepped towards my mother. As at our parting so long ago, she said not one word. She turned and passed through the open gate. I followed, my heart racing. I passed through the narrow gap, the metal frames towering above me. The gate swung closed behind me with a resounding clang. Mr Roberts pushed his key into the lock and the heavy metal lever swung across with a thud that seemed to echo across the bay stretched out in front of me, under the wide, open sky, dotted with gulls circling silently on the swelling currents of air.

Chapter 16: Ten Shillings

I did not know where the long walk would take us. We set off down the long, straight road. I kept close to the wall by my side, fearful of the wide open space out across the bay. We headed along towards the towering chimneys of the power station and back past the horses and their laden carts. The wind off the bay whipped up the black dust from the road, stinging my eyes. Gradually, the Pigeon House dropped back further from view as we turned away from the bay, and headed back into the city.

I carried my parcel under my arm and strode along behind mother. The pennies clinked in my pocket and rubbed against the tops of my legs. The string from the parcel began to cut into my fingers, so I swapped hands as we went.

The streets began to narrow and the buildings were larger again. There were many more people about and the noise of all the comings and goings was thumping into my head. Mother weaved about between the people around me and I hurried to keep up. I kept close to her as we crossed busy streets, and turned along unfamiliar routes. The boots began to cut into the back of my ankles.

We turned into a narrow, dark ally. Along the left, a flaking wall with windows and doorways. Above us, poles jutting out into the air with clothes swaying gently in the breeze. On the other side of me a high wall, shutting out light from the windows opposite. Mother swung into one of the doorways. I followed up the narrow steps inside, and we entered the room.

It was gloomy. One window, opposite the door, was slightly open, letting in the din of the street at the end of the narrow passage. I could hear voices, shouts and calls. The overcoats were tossed across the bed. The place felt musty. I stood and looked around, turning slightly as my eyes drifted from wall to brown wall.

I asked if I could see Lizzie again, now that I was back home. Mother stood still a while, her hands set firmly on her hips, as she looked me up and down.

"She's gone," she eventually replied, speaking quickly and firmly, her face set hard.

I sensed this meant for ever. I knew I would never be seeing her again. My head dropped and I felt the room closing around me.

"Now, we'll get these things off you."

She took the parcel and placed it on the wooden chair. She lifted my arms up and peeled off my jumper. She knelt down to undo the laces of my boots and slid them off my feet. She undid the buckle on the trousers and they dropped to the floor weighed down by the contents of the pockets. She folded the clothes up on top of the package on the chair, placing the boots on top. She sat me on the bed and passed over some rags that I recalled my brothers wearing when they had climbed over the wall to visit me. I pulled them over me, and sat cross-legged on the bed.

My younger brothers, who had scaled the wall at the Pigeon House, burst into the room. Instantly they bombarded me with questions.

"Have you brought any food with you? Did they give you any money? Why have they sent you back?"

My answers were cut off by further agitated questions, until the torrent slowed, and I began recounting how I came to leave. They sat attentively, looking at me. They listened as I recounted the shape of my days in the Pigeon House, and told them again about Bridie, the lovely girl from the city who had cared for me until she simply disappeared one day.

"Why did she go?" they chorused after I had explained all the little things she had done for me.

"'What happened to her?"

I began to think about her again. Her nice face, her little laugh, and the gentle and reassuring pat on my hand whenever she left my bedside. And I sensed again the desolation after her disappearance, and how the Sisters had averted their eyes when they answered my questions about her. My brothers listened attentively as I told them about the clothes she brought me that first Christmas, and how she gradually brought them back to me after Sister Aloysius had taken them away. They made me describe the clothes again. And they wanted to know if they could see them.

I turned towards the chair across the room, where mother had placed them. The parcel and the clothes were no longer there. And mother was nowhere to be seen.

I suddenly felt cold. I thought back to the nights before I had left the city, when we had been sent out to find her, slumped somewhere in the corner of an ale house, reeking of drink.

That night was to be the same. And the night after, and the one after that. At McGee's Court, I was back home, to an empty place, a space of nothingness. Back with no clothes, no pennies, no food and no bed of my own. And the constant, numbing drum beat in my head of the dark memories that I could not bring out into the light.

Mother came back eventually. She was slumped again on the bed, wailing her way through a song I seemed to remember from years before, the words as indistinct as ever, punctuated by cursing and yelling. She repeated it over a few times, until collapsing in a stupor. She was clutching a single sheet of paper in her hand. I went over to look at it. It was a song sheet, collected from the ale house, stained a bit, but carrying the right words of the song she had been slurring through for the last hour or so. 'Johnny, I hardly knew ye'. I took the sheet out of her damp hand and folded it carefully, hiding it under a box by the bed.

"There'll be no more schooling, not after what happened before," father said, the next morning.

"You have to get out to work, same as me. Same as the others." He mentioned no names.

I was back, living on the streets, just as before. Back to the old ways of scavenging and begging wherever I could, and collecting scraps to sell for pennies. I thought about John, and remembered the whispered conversations we had had in the yard all those years ago, when he had talked about England

and his escape. Again, I saw him, proud and tall, looking distinguished in the uniform I saw him wearing. There was his wavy hair again and his jaunty smile. 'It's the only way, the only way'. Those words of his echoed again in my mind.

Images of him, and memories of the things he had said to me, played about in my mind as I sat on the kerb stone, splashing my feet in the running water by the drain, and waiting for the stall holders to reach the end of trading. The time when the best scraps would appear. I dreamt of John, standing back before me, beckoning to me, as he came to gather me up in his arms and take me with him, back to England.

Father had simply said I should work. But all I could see before me at the moment was the life of the street, the begging, the scrounging, and the careful harbouring of pennies and crusts.

I told Aunt Kitty what he had said. She scrunched her face and shook her head, then said she would talk to my uncle and see what he could do for me. Maybe there was something that could be sorted out. She would see what she could do. She handed me a large crust of bread, with a mug of tea and said I should stay here that night as he was expected to come by the next morning. I snuggled down, ready for a comforting sleep.

I sensed the air about me suddenly go cold. There was a wind whipping its way over me, making the sheet on top of me rise and fall, flapping about. A dull red light was swaying about above me, casting strange shadows across the room and over my bed. I was turning and turning, wrestling again in the darkness and reaching out. And then for a brief moment I was still again. Then the hand was there, clawing about, cold, sliding around. Again I turned, but as I did so there was no movement in my body. Only the hand was moving, working its way about, and hurting me, making me sting and burn. There was a hot breath moving close to me, piercing through the cold air. And streaks of white flashed about.

I reached out for the little shape of carved wood and its precious statue. I stretched out as far as I could. My arm was hurting. I went forward towards it, further still, but it slowly moved away from me, always just out of reach. The pieces of coloured paper fluttered away and the stones rolled to the side. The arch in the wood was laid open before me, a feint glow coming from inside. I reached and reached but I could not touch her. The pain beneath me made me spin about and I lost sight of the arch.

I could hear her calling after me, through the darkness but no sound would come as my throat tightened inside me. It was coming into me, reaching right into me and making me explode inside. The pain lifted me, and the shapes around me melted, as my eyes opened, to see Aunt Kitty, across the room, still sleeping, with the gentle rise and fall of the sheet laid out over her. I felt my pounding heart begin to slow, and, with the back of my hand, I wiped the beads of sweat from my forehead. And realised what I had to do.

"Well maybe he could help out with the peat," he said, looking over at me, the next morning.

Aunt Kitty and my uncle were sat at her little table, each with a mug of tea.

"An extra pair of hands would help, after all. I'll take him there today and we'll see what he can manage."

The peat was in piles around the yard, some of it on racks drying out. There was a table by the entrance bearing a large set of scales and various cylindrical weights. He showed me how the peat was cut up, and how the scales worked. I learned how to balance the peat slices on one of the pans and the weights on the other, until the red needle was centrally positioned over the numbers on the white panel in the middle. He gave me several coppers at the end of each day. I asked Aunt Kitty if I could keep them safe with her, rather than take them home.

I realised how far away I was, back home, from the reassurance that I had seen in Bridie's face. The nightmares kept recurring. My need intensified. Somehow I needed my shield again.

I told mother I needed to be confirmed.

She looked at me, then headed for the door.

"I suppose so," she said, as she stepped out of the room, pulling the door shut behind her.

I waited several days for mother to say what would now happen, but she came back with nothing. When I tried to raise the matter again, I could see her winding up for a rage, and so I let it go. Father said I would have to ask mother about it.

There were steep steps up to the large grey door. I had seen the nuns hurrying in and out of the building, which was only just across the street from our room. I reached up to the metal handle and yanked it up and own. A few moments later, I heard a bolt slide on the other side of the door, which then slowly opened before me, to reveal a short, plump nun, with little wire-rimmed spectacles perched half way along her thin nose.

"Well, yes, we do have confirmation classes here. But we will have to enrol you and I will need to see Mother Superior about it."

They explained to me that the classes were held twice a week and it was essential that I attended them all. I couldn't skip off if I felt like it. They were an hour at a time, in the early evening. I worked out that I could get back to the building in time after helping my uncle out with the peat weighing.

The words I knew. But here they were softer. The same words, when coming from Father Roach at my school, had been harsh and biting. They had snapped at me. Father Thorne had used the same words too. They sounded an echo in my mind, and sometimes I saw the waving walls of his tin chapel and felt him next to me, urging me on with the words, over and over until he was willing to let me run back out into the yard, and into the light.

These were the words I had used when hunched in front of the wooden arch, my hands clenched so tight that they hurt.

But now they settled around me with an ease, like the evening light that came through the coloured windows in the room where I received my instructions. I felt sure the words offered me a way.

After months of classes, a tall, imposing figure of a man stood before us.

"The Archbishop is here to explain to you everything about the confirmation ceremony and what you are going to need, so listen carefully now."

He spoke with a deep, low voice. I listened as he explained the ceremony, the need for all of us to appear at our very smartest, and the round of family visits that would follow so that we could announce our confirmation and receive the blessings of all those who loved and cared for us.

I thought about the smart clothes I had been wearing on the day I left the Pigeon House and saw myself parading about in them after the grand confirmation ceremony. Then I looked down at my tatty rags, and recalled the sudden disappearance of the brown parcel and the clothes that I had worn with such pride. And sensed a wide gap open up between me and the instructions still being intoned by the Archbishop.

"Well, we'll just have to go the Priory and see what they can do for us," was all mother could say, as I patiently explained the need for proper clothes.

After some days of pleading, we eventually made our way over to the grand building in White Friar

Street.   Mother wrapped on the door.   It was opened after a while. He stood there peering down at us, the tall, gaunt familiar shape, the cold stare cast down into my upturned eyes.

"Well you can't present him like that!" snapped Father Roach, after listening to my mother's explanation, "that's for sure."

"Yes, he will need proper clothes, I know," mother responded, "but we can't afford any and that's why we've come for your help, Father."

He sighed.

"Wait here. I'll see what we can do."

He moved back inside the door, closing it slowly, the latch clicking softly as it came to rest. Mother lent back against the wall, her arms folded across her chest. I sat on the step opposite, trying hard to avoid her eyes. I ran the imploring words through my head, over and over.

The latch rattled and the door opened again. Father Roach held out his clenched hand towards my mother, who stepped forward to receive it.

"Here, this is all we can offer now, do what you can with this."

She unfolded the little piece of paper and peered down at it.

"Ten shillings! Is that it? Is this how I'm supposed to fit him up for a confirmation? How do you expect me to..."

He cut her off in mid flow.

"Like I said, this all we have now. Do what you can with it."

I could feel the rage swelling. I stood back against the wall.

"Well if that's all you can do, you can stick your confirmation", she screamed out as he closed the door in her face. She swung round quickly and shouted at me.

"Come on. We're going."

I hurried along behind her as she stormed off along the road, her fingers rolling the note around as she went. The ground seemed to strike at the soles of my feet as we hurried along through the streets. I heard the words running through my mind again, but they seemed to be jumbled now. The flow and the rhythm wasn't there anymore. There were sounds but without shape. As I looked around me I saw doors closing, and people turning away, going about their business. Mother pushed her way through the oncoming crowds. I caught glimpses of her between the figures in front of me, until she suddenly darted to one side, disappearing into a dingy room where, from outside, I could hear cackles of laugher and the shouting of voices, drowning out the singing.

I sat on the curb, the cold earth creeping through my thin pants, making me shiver. The wheels of a cart rattled past close to my face, sending a shower of dust and little stones up into the air, which peppered my ankles as they fell back to the ground.

Chapter 17: A Song Book

I looked up from the gutter and over, across the road. People scurried along and the noises of the city whirled about under the heavy grey sky. In amongst the bustle, there was a figure standing still. A tall smartly dressed man, carrying a large grey kit bag in one arm. He was looking straight at me. Wavy hair peeked out from under his cap. I stared, uncertain and not believing. My pulse began to race.

He crossed the road and stood in front of me. I peered up into his face.

"Lorcán, is that you?"

There he stood before me, tears rolling down his cheeks and dripping down onto his smart jacket. John stretched out his hand and levered me up from the gutter. I stumbled as I rose, my legs unable to carry me. He steadied me, taking a firm hold of my arm.

"Are you taking me back to England?" I gasped through my own tears.

For a while he said nothing, just holding me by the arm and staring down at my rags and bare feet. He wiped his tears with the back of his hand. With his kit bag slung over one shoulder, and me hanging tight to his other arm, we headed back in the direction of our room. He said nothing as we went, but kept looking over to me, down into my expectant face and watery eyes.

John stood before my shaken mother. She eyed him over and looked uncertainly at his smart clothes and the grey kit bag now down on the floor beside his shiny brown boots.

They began an uneasy conversation, mother falling into periods of sullen silence, then powering up into angry accusation about him not supporting her any more, leaving her to struggle along, taking up with the British, turning his back; and on it went, ranging randomly over stony ground. John doing his best to stay calm and cool her bubbling rages.

"So I'll be stopping a bit, ma. I'm going to take a look around before going back."

Mother raged on at him, until finally pulling on her coat and storming out of the room, slamming the door behind her as she went. Responding to my persistent questioning, John finally opened up his kit bag and carefully he laid out in front of me his smart army uniform. The brown jacket had bright polished buttons. The trousers had a fine line down the side and a wide, polished belt clasped together by a bright, shining buckle which glinted in the light. He talked excitedly about his life in England and in the army. He said he was going to get married and explained how he was planning a new life when his time in the army was over. Then he said we should go together into the city. There were things he needed to get. He folded his uniform away, stowing it neatly in the kit bag, which he rested up against the wall in the corner of the room.

Gesturing to me to follow, we left the room, heading out across the yard and into the busy street. I picked up my questioning about England and he patiently answered me, describing the wide streets, the great buildings and the new life he was leading. I saw myself at his side, walking those streets with him. The two of us proud and strong.

He eventually steered the conversation away from my persistent questions. I followed him around as we went through the streets, waiting anxiously every now and then outside shops until he would reappear.

Wearily, we eventually made our way back to our room. We turned into the ally. We smelt smoke as we approached the entrance to the yard. As we did, mother's back quickly disappeared into the doorway, a long stick hanging down from one hand.

Smoke rose silently from a small heap in the corner of the courtyard. We went across to inspect it. Amongst the smouldering ashes of his uniform, I could see the belt buckle, it's bold shape blackened and standing out against the dull red glow underneath.

The fight that erupted was fierce. I fled from the room, tearfully wending my way through the streets back to Aunt Kitty's. She produced warming tea, and listened attentively, her head shaking slowly from side to side as I recounted the fateful consequences of John's unexpected return. Again, I stayed, too afraid to go back to witness the rolling confrontation between John and my mother.

"Mr McGuire says he will take you on at the dairy. He needs some help with the deliveries. It's nearer home and I think he can pay you a bit more than I can."

My uncle explained that he had been asking around and had found me something else to do instead of helping him out at the peat yard.

Lucan Dairies was close to our room and the early start was easier as a result. Mr McGuire was a short, neat man, in a light brown overcoat. He showed me the cart that the milk had to be loaded onto. He placed a small step near the end of the cart, where a section folded down towards the floor. The metal crates were stacked close by. He took hold of a crate and swung it up onto the back of the cart, pushing it hard, making it slide along the wooden slats which formed the loading area.

I took hold of one of the crates and heaved it across towards the step, where I quickly set it down, my arms pulling. I clambered up onto the step, standing at the side of the crate. I then grasped both sides of it and heaved it up over the lip of the cart and onto the loading area.

"Going to take a bit of practice is this," said Mr McGuire, looking doubtfully at my skinny arms.

"Maybe you'd be better dropping the bottles off on the doorsteps, at least to start with. We'll get her hitched up and see how we go."

He disappeared across the yard, returning after a while leading by the reins a huge grey horse, which was tossing its head about as if trying to break free from his grip. He led the animal round to the front of the cart and proceeded to lift the side arms, strapping them onto a heavy leather harness slung over the beast's back.

We clambered up onto the rough wooden seat at the front of the cart. Tugging at the reins, Mr McGuire jerked the animal into action. The cart suddenly moved forward, making the bottles in the crates behind us clink loudly as the wheels bounced over the cobbles.

I learned to reach back for the bottles, gathering one in each hand, move to the side of the seat and drop down to the ground as we slowed up outside each house. Gradually the cart load was delivered, and Mr McGuire turned us back towards the dairy, the great horse setting off at a terrifying gallop, making me grab hold of my seat as tightly as I could in order to avoid spilling down into the street below.

The beast continued to scare me. It seemed beyond Mr McGuire's ability to control it. With no obvious provocation, it was prone at times to rear up on its hind legs, causing the cart behind us to tip back with a sudden lurch, sending milk bottles rolling about and crashing to the ground. Mr McGuire fought valiantly with the reins and tried to steady the flighty animal as best he could, bringing it finally to a standstill, after which I would scurry back to retrieve what I could of our precious load, and to sweep the shattered glass into the gutter.

It seemed a perilous way to earn my ten shillings a week. My nervousness around the beast seemed to goad it to yet more dramatic outburst of uncontrolled energy.

John was leaving, sooner than planned. He and mother could not even speak. He came into the room simply to announce that he was going back to England. He declared very steadily that he would never be returning.

I rushed out of the room after him, pleading through tears to go with him, back to England.

"Look, it isn't possible," he said choking.

"There's rules. You can't just go, like that. And you can't come into the army anyway, you're too young."

"You need to work, like I did. Save some money up. Keep it away from mother. Then you have to get a permit. But I'll be there. I'll wait for you. But come as soon as you can. It's the only way."

He tore himself away from my clutching arm, and swinging his bag up over his broad shoulder, walked away, unable to look back at me. I crumpled to the floor, shaking with the tears that streamed from my eyes, finally curling up in a heap where I was, lying, quivering and whimpering until the light faded and the night air bit once again into my exposed limbs. I stared up, and through reddened eyes, gazed at the stars in the clearing sky above. Then, slowly, I climbed the narrow stairs back to the room, entering as quietly as I could, and slipping my aching body under a corner of the overcoat.

"I hear O'Connor is taking over his father's old dairy business," Mr McGuire said to me one day back in the yard, after we had endured another day of erratic and uncontrollable behaviour by the horse.

"I don't think he's planning on using horses and carts," he added with a grin.

"I reckon you should go over and see if he'll take you on."

His yard was also close to our room. I went there the next morning. I got there early. I looked about for someone to approach but the place was quiet. I walked across the yard to a low building with a line of little windows along its side and a wooden door at the end, which was half open. I peered in. I could see a large lady in a white piny, her hair tied tightly back behind her head. She was counting out eggs, placing them quickly into trays set out on the table in front of her.

After a while she saw me.

"You the lad from McGuire's?" she said, still counting out the eggs.

I nodded.

"Been expecting you," she continued.

"Come over here, let's have a look at you."

She fired more questions at me about the rounds I did with Mr McGuire and about how long I had been there and why I wasn't going to stay. She nodded quietly, still counting out the eggs, as she listened to my woeful tales about the uncontrollable horse.

"Right," she said in the end, "run along now, come back first thing tomorrow, we'll get you started."

She carried on quickly dispersing the eggs into their trays as I left the room, relieved at the prospect of my relocation and no further encounters with Mr McGuire's nightmare of a horse.

I turned up at Mr O'Connor's dairies at half past six the next morning. The yard foreman saw me enter past the open gate. He marched across to me.

"Where do you think you're going?" he barked.

He looked me up and down.

"Can't work here without boots boy. Be off home. Come back when you're dressed right."

He waved me out of the yard, watching me carefully as I retreated from his sight.

Dejectedly, I walked away from the yard, once again recalling the reassuring feel of the clothes around me on the day I walked out of the Pigeon House. Clothes that quickly disappeared, leaving me once again in the rags which had stood as a barrier to confirmation, and now to the work which father insisted I had, and which I wanted, knowing now that it was the only way to follow John to England.

I soon tracked down the nearest street traders and started, once again, to lie in wait for the end of the day, gathering the scraps from the floor and begging for the better leftovers. The bucket loads still found a ready buyer needing to feed pigs and I slowly collected up the pennies. They were sufficient for an adequate pair of boots, even though the sole of one was split, letting the damp in when the ground was wet. But from the top they looked alright. Enough to get me past the yard foreman.

I collected the money stored away at Aunt Kitty's and went to the pawn shop which was mother's regular haunt. I had enough to get hold of decent but basic clothes that looked strong enough and thick enough to sustain me through whatever weather would beat down on my soon to be resumed milk rounds.

Reclad, I returned as soon as I could to the dairy. I marched in, passing close by the foreman, who watched me silently as I stepped passed in my newly acquired boots. He watched me keenly, saying nothing, as I headed for Mr O'Connor's office.

He gave me patient and gentle instruction about how he wanted to build the business and how I could help him. He seemed kindly, speaking softly and slowly and punctuating his words from time to time with a quick smile and a little flick of his head.

Under his careful watch, I began loading the carts, counting out the crates as we went, to match the number with the order read out by a man who stood by with a clip board and a pencil. I bumped the crates down onto the platform of the cart, the little one-third pint bottles jostling against their metal holders. Each new crate pushed the previous one a little farther along the platform until the loading area was full.

The first Friday came and he placed twelve shillings into my hand. Mother had found out what the rate was and was fierce in her response if I handed her anything much under that amount later that day. She left later, carrying her shopping bag, promising a good meal for us all. She didn't return until gone midnight, waking us as she clambered up the stairs, bursting into the room, followed by two other women as drunk and as chaotic as she was.

They swung around the room, as groans and shouts emerged from the bed where we were huddled together. A fierce argument began and then subsided as she stopped herself from toppling over by grabbing hold of her companions' ample arm. They swayed about together for a while, the third laughing loudly at their predicament. Then she began to sing, one arm held out with her hand flat against the wall to steady her as she recited her uncertain way through the words of 'The little shirt my mother made for me', clasped tightly in her swaying hand. Her companions made up the chorus as mother worked her way through the verses in random order. Exhausted, she collapsed to the floor. Crawling across the room, I retrieved the paper from her hand and stowed it carefully with the other.

"You should be able to manage this now," the yard foreman said after a few weeks of loading.

He led me across to a black bicycle lent up against the wall. It had the dairy's name painted on a plate fixed above the chain. There were metal racks over the wheels, each big enough to take a crate of bottles. He wheeled me about the yard, holding on under the saddle. My legs just reached down to the ground, extended to full tip-toe. Slowly, I got the sense of balance and began to circle the yard in a wobbly but upright fashion.

He loaded crates on, first one on the back, and I wobbled off again. Then one on the front. The effort to move the bike along was considerable but I could make just enough progress to keep everything upright. He told me about a group of streets not too far away from the yard and explained how much milk needed delivering to each in the morning. With the black bike and its heavy load, I began my own milk round.

At the end of the narrow ally running down to the door which led to our stairs, someone had dumped an old sack, tied across the top with some rough string. The sack bulged out in odd shapes, looking as if they were trying to burst their way out. I ran my fingers over the protrusions, wondering what they were. I dug my fingers into the knotted string and began to prise it apart. It yielded to my effort and fell away. I pulled open the top of the sack and peered in. It was smelly, possibly I thought because of rotten food in there somewhere. Pulling aside the scrunched paper at the top I felt further down. There was something solid, at the side where I had seen the odd shape jutting out. I got my fingers onto it and pulled it out, past a few bottles that clanked together as I disturbed them with my arm.

I pulled the object out. It was brown and stained a bit and smelt very musty. I opened it up. It wasn't quite the book Aunt Kitty had used in my early reading lessons, but it was something similar. The brown, stained pages had lots of words printed closely all over. I leafed through it. All pages the same. I guessed it was a very long story. I brushed the cover with my hands and picked off a few bits that had stuck to it from other items inside the sack. I had a book and a use in mind.

Now that I had a delivery round, and it was steadily growing, the dairy put a little bit more money in my hand on a Friday. I kept the difference a secret from mother. I saved the few extra pennies each week and stored them in secret places and at Aunt Kitty's, where I could feel sure mother would not find them.

The dairy began to use vans and the foreman said I could leave the bike some days and go out on the bigger rounds that the vehicles covered and help the driver, Mr Halpin. We loaded up to 40 crates in the van early in the morning. I ran up and down the steps of the big houses, dropping the bottles by the door and learning to bring back the empty ones, hooked onto my fingers. By the time of the afternoon round, I was tired. When the delivery was to the back of the house, I looked to see if the door was open. Some houses offered what I was looking for.

Mr Halpin and I stood at the open doorway, empty bottles clanking in one hand, signalling our presence. We were waved in, and took a seat at the table. Hot tea was warming. Soup, even better. The milk round provided the nourishment to help us get through the arduous day, and made up for the shortage of meals I encountered at home, especially at the beginning of the week. The food from the kitchens of the big houses began to rebuild the lost strength in my body.

Mother was certainly in the ale house. It was Saturday. I pulled the song pages out from their secure hiding place and unfolded them, smoothing them out with the palm of my hand. I read through the words and hummed what I knew of the tune. I went outside, down the stairs and across the yard, to the place where I had hidden the little brown book. I took it back inside and opened it out on the table. Carefully I pressed the song sheet down onto the open page, securing it with some glue which I had found at the dairy. I added decorations to the page, cut from newspapers and cigarette packets. I began my song book. And kept it safe, well away from anyone who would find other uses for it.

The large window gleamed in the sunlight and I had to press one hand up against the glass and shield my face so that I could look through. The suits were really smart, and came in a large variety of colours and patterns. I looked carefully at each one in the display, and at the prices pinned lightly to the lapels.

The assistant explained the payment terms that were promoted in the window, looking me up and down uncertainly.

"I think we may have them in your size," he said.

I penned my name down on a piece of paper he pushed across the counter towards me and noted in my mind that I needed to come back with at least six pence each Friday, ideally a shilling, if I could manage it.

"I wonder if you could do me a little favour", she said, as I dropped off a couple of bottles of milk at the little fruit shop opposite the diary.

"I've got to nip off for a minute. Can you mind the shop?"

As this was the last drop of the round, I agreed, and slid in behind the counter, casting my eye over the tasty looking fruit.

"Won't be a minute," she said, disappearing behind the shop door.

I breathed in the smell of the rosy fruit and ran my fingers over the shining surface of a green apple. It all smelt and tasted good and I imagined lands of such bounty, far away.

She reappeared at the door.

"Thanks love, thanks," she said quickly as she took her piny down from its hook and began tying it around her waist.

"Here, have an apple, and this for your trouble."

She pressed sixpence into my hand. I left, biting eagerly into the juicy apple and pledging the sixpence to my suit fund.

Another cold winter made the milk round that little more arduous as we pressed our way through ice and snow, the little van slipping about and the biting wind whipping into our faces as we hurried to each door way. The open kitchen doors were especially welcoming in such weather and the soup provided essential nourishment. I looked after the fruit shop more regularly and the sixpences accelerated the rate of contribution to the suit fund.

On the day that I nervously walked back to the shop, where I had pressed my face to the glass so many months before, I clutched in my hand the final sixpence needed to secure it. The measuring had been done weeks before, the tape running from head to foot, around my chest and along my legs and arms. The lad had murmured little numbers and jotted things down with a pencil on his pad. It made me think of the excitement I felt all those years ago when the little parcels of clothing were brought to me at that first Christmas in the Pigeon House, after the Sisters had played games with me, swinging tapes around me. With a shiver, I also remembered how short a time I kept hold of them.

"Will you wear it or shall I fold it up and wrap it?"

After such a long wait it seemed a strange question. I pulled on the trousers and admired them in the mirror. I slipped my arms back into sleeves being held open for me by the assistant. I did up a button, then undid it, and turned about in front of the mirror, finally doing it up again.

I walked proudly, thinking everyone was looking at me. Even the scuffed boots I wore for the dairy work did not detract from the fine appearance I knew I made as I took a long route back home.

My brothers were certainly impressed and looked the suit up and own as I turned around in front of them. I thought it was as good enough to wear for joining John in England. They agreed. I needed to keep it in good shape if I was to follow him. I took it off reluctantly and laid it out on the bed, carefully placing the hanger that the shop had given me up inside the top of the jacket. I hooked it up over a nail in the wall. I wanted father to admire it when he got back from work. I said nothing to my brothers about the real purpose of the suit. I just said it would help me get a better job. I told them to keep an eye on it. I had to go to mind the fruit shop. I was going to take the suit away once father had seen it.

"I'll not be long."

She closed the door of the fruit shop behind her as usual and my brief spell in charge late in the evening began once again. I began sorting the boxes behind the counter, cleaning out the little scraps of tissue paper and flattening them out into a pile on the counter. The boxes stacked easily and looked neater than when strewn around in the back room. Some damaged fruit was scattered about on the surface of the table in the back room, and I began clearing it up, dropping the pieces into one of the crates. The shop was looking really tidy.

I started to feel familiar pangs of hunger, and realised that she had been gone much longer than usual, past the time when I knew she generally closed up for the night. I sat on an upturned box and kicked my heels against the thin wooden slats, wondering what had happened to her. It had been dark for some time, when the door swung open.

"Ah, sorry about that. Terrible commotion out there. Some dreadful fight or something. Couldn't get back for the crowds. Run along, you must be starving. I'll settle up tomorrow."

Wednesday was usually a good dinner. I climbed the stairs in anticipation, up towards the ever-present drip, putting my weary hand on the door knob and entering the room. They sat dejectedly at the table, staring at me as I looked about, wondering why there was no smell of cooking on the stove and no sign of mother. Or of my suit.

She came back sometime in the early morning, again wailing at the top of her voice, screeching as she banged about on the staircase, bursting onto the room and weaving her way across to the wall opposite the door. A version of 'Beautiful dreamer' poured forth, as I pulled the coat tighter over me, and clamped my hands over my head. I rescued the song sheet the next morning, from its position stuffed between the mounds of damp peat next to the stove.

"What do I need to get to England?"

Wearily, the man in the grubby white shirt sat opposite me began to talk about permits and orders and rules and regulations and proofs and guarantees and all manner of things that sailed over me rather like my early school lessons.

"Look," he said seeing my glazed expression, "have you got a job promised you? No job promise, no permit. That is it basically."

"Now why on earth would you want to be doing that?" demanded Mr O'Connor, the dairy boss.

"Why go to England when you're building up a fine little round here? I can make it bigger for you and you will earn good money, you know."

I sat in our room, staring at the blank wall and the protruding nail, proclaiming its emptiness to me. The plan began to take shape in my head. How long it would take to save again. How I could spirit up a job offer to get me past the man at the permit office. How I could leave all this behind me. I turned it over in my head, over and over again, trying to make it come right. To make sense. I looked around the dingy room trying to make sense of the nothingness that surrounded me. And I saw John's figure. Waiting.

Whatever it takes, I resolved. Whatever it takes.

Chapter 18: Time

Mr O'Connor continued in his efforts to talk me out of it. He insisted I could do well in his business. He was willing to offer me bigger rounds and more money. He was happy to bring one of my brothers into the business too, to work alongside me. Together, we could build it up, he said.

But the pull was irresistible. Even the regular knockbacks at the permit office would not dent my resolve. Time and again, the officials shook their heads, saying I had a good job, there was no reason for me to go. And there was no job offer in England. They would not issue the permit. Final. That was that.

But no barrier was going to hold me back. Not any longer. The way out was clear and I was taking it.

I worked away at the dairy, continuing to ignore Mr O'Connor's pleas and his financial inducements. Between shifts, I was quietly making my plans and preparing for the day. I resolved a way to make it happen. At last.

I peered at the picture on the front of the document. I looked like a scrunched up little boy, with untidy black hair, looking miserable and tiny, drowning in the over-sized blue coat Mr O'Connor had given me. But that was the picture they put in the travel warrant, and which I now held in my trembling hand.

There was no job offer. No plan for that had come to anything. So I was to be a tourist, as far as the authorities were concerned, with a three-month pass. But one I knew was travelling on a one-way ticket. Now it was no dream any more. I was about to break from it all, run out of the darkness, burst open the gates and take hold of the outstretched hand.

I had saved enough money all over again now to get some clothes fit for the journey and the ticket for the boat. All hidden away, well out of mother's reach. I kept looking at the permit, trying to make sense of all the tiny print and examining the perforations that ran along its edge. Just a piece of printed paper, not unlike many I had pasted into my brown book. But it had a value I seemed unable to measure. I kept it tucked carefully inside the travel warrant, itself hidden between the pages of the little brown book.

I bought a small cardboard case, covered to look like leather, but in truth rather flimsy, with a simple little catch to keep the lid and contents secure. With the last of the money I had, I bought a large piece of bacon and a big slab of butter, and I had both wrapped up tight in paper and cloth to preserve them. The best currency I knew for repaying those in faraway England who would get my new life started. I packed them into the case. I kept it hidden away from view, together with the clothes that would carry me off in the morning.

I finished the Saturday shift at Mr O'Connor's dairy. I crossed the street in the settling evening gloom and wound my way up the stair to the room. For the last time. I slept only fitfully, glancing in my waking moments at my younger brothers stretched out under the coats, watching them turn and wriggle as they tried to hold in the warmth.

In the morning, it was time. At last.

I could not imagine why there were tears in my mother's eyes as I boarded the train to take me down to the port. Father, also tearful, silently watched me clamber into the carriage, my little head waving loosely about between the upturned sides of the high collar on my coat. Clutching the brown case, I stared through the grimy window at the city buildings beside the station, dark, towering up into the sky over the side of the train.

The train slowly pulled away. I saw their two figures, diminished, standing on the platform edge. I watched the city retreat as the train gathered speed and moved out to nearer the bay. I felt the journey I had planned for so long drawing closer now, as the carriage rocked its way along the twisting track.

The noise and bustle of the port greeted me as I stepped out after the short ride. I followed signs for the Hollyhead boat, and joined a noisy crowd jostling their way towards a steep gang plank which rose up towards the edge of a boat, already issuing clouds of grey smoke from its funnel. I hauled myself up the plank, one arm clutching my bag, the other gripping tight to the slippery rail. I made the big step down onto the deck of the boat and looked around.

People milling about, many with big cases, some even with wheels. A lot of shouting and waving, aimed back to the shore, and children clutching nervously to their mothers' hand. Everyone chatting and busy about something.

I wandered about the deck, dodging out the way of people hurrying from one place to the next. Finding a quieter spot towards the front, I sat down on the deck, arranging the coat underneath me as a cushion against the hard wooden floor. I could peer through the railings, down onto the quayside. The vibrations in the deck beneath me increased and, looking up, I saw thicker grey smoke belching out above my head. There was more shouting, and great ropes were hauled up, their ends dripping as they slid across the deck towards the slowly spinning capstan. The crowds on the quay grew smaller, as the boat began to pull away and the wind in my face grew stronger as the speed steadily increased.

The city began to slip away at my side. Out across the bay, I could see the thin, tall chimney of the power station, its black smoke caught by the wind and chased around in a low swirl. There, down beside it I could see a long low wall stretching the whole length of the shore line, descending to a thin ribbon of rocks, splashed white by the lapping tide. And above it, set in another wall, further back, a pair of large black gates, locked shut.

It must have been the increasing wind blowing hard into my face that watered my eyes. I turned my head down and wiped them dry with the sleeve of the great coat. There at my feet, the little brown case. I picked it up and set it on my lap, and clicked open the lid. The packets of food nestled snugly in place and there, wedged in beside, the only other possession coming with me on my journey.

I pulled it out and began leafing through its pages. Against the noise of the churning engines and the droning of the wind in my ears, I hummed along to the words,

*"Why stand I here like a ghost and a shadow?
'Tis time I was moving, 'tis time I passed on."*

Afterword

The return to Dublin Bay came fifty years later when it was Larry, now, in the company of his wife and family who made the long walk by the low south wall towards the gates that marked the entrance to where the Pigeon House had once been.

The Pigeon House had silently haunted him, nestling down in the memory of a retreating childhood. Then, looking into the faces of his own children, it would gather itself and step forward again.

Drawn by the bitter, painful memories of that place, he was now finally able to retrace the steps that had taken him there as a barefoot, ragged, weakened child, his lungs ravaged by tuberculosis — another victim of the infection that tore through the city throughout that time, propelled on its way by the mix of poverty, squalor, infestation and overcrowding.

Another journey had begun the day he sailed out, past those gates, headed, at last, for England.

A journey taking him to his brother's early support, to lodging rooms, and finally into work. Years of assiduous attendance at night school slowly filled the gaps in his fractured and limited education, finally providing the groundings for his long, successful years of rewarding work.

It was the journey of the rest of his life, anchored ultimately by the sure and certain foundation of his loving home, his wife, his two sons, his daughter, and his grandchildren.

But the Pigeon House, far away over the vast stretches of water, on a distant shore, tugged at the anchor.

The true scale of that chasm between his past and his present only came fully into view as he stood at those gates, his mind filling with remorse for all the poor souls who suffered on the other side, so few surviving, never to walk out through those gates, back into the light.

How tragic and how painful it had been.   How warped, the line of care. On the other side of those gates, the way left clear for those who worked out their own tawdry self-gratification, concealed and unchallenged, protected under a blanket of divine authority.   While those driven by sympathy and compassion had been cast out.

The distance between then and now had always been pulling away at his certainties. And he knew the only thing to do was to begin to close the gap, *by bringing the memories that lay beyond those gates out into the open spaces of his world.*

After the return, the words would only come slowly, painfully pulling at their roots as they moved from then to now, landing on the page before him. So slowly, the bridge was built and the story unfolded, sometimes shared, sometimes solitary, as it reached out to join the two opposing shores.

In the end they linked. The story emerged, its long course finally run. He seemed to draw a reassuring peace as we sat together, talking it through, slotting in the final pieces of the picture. His strong, clear, steady recall, reaching out, back across all the years, splashed with the tears of pain.

It was the only way he could do it.

He passed through the gates, triumphantly, in May 2011, in his eightieth year.

Printed in Great Brit.
by Amazon.co.uk, L
Marston Gate.